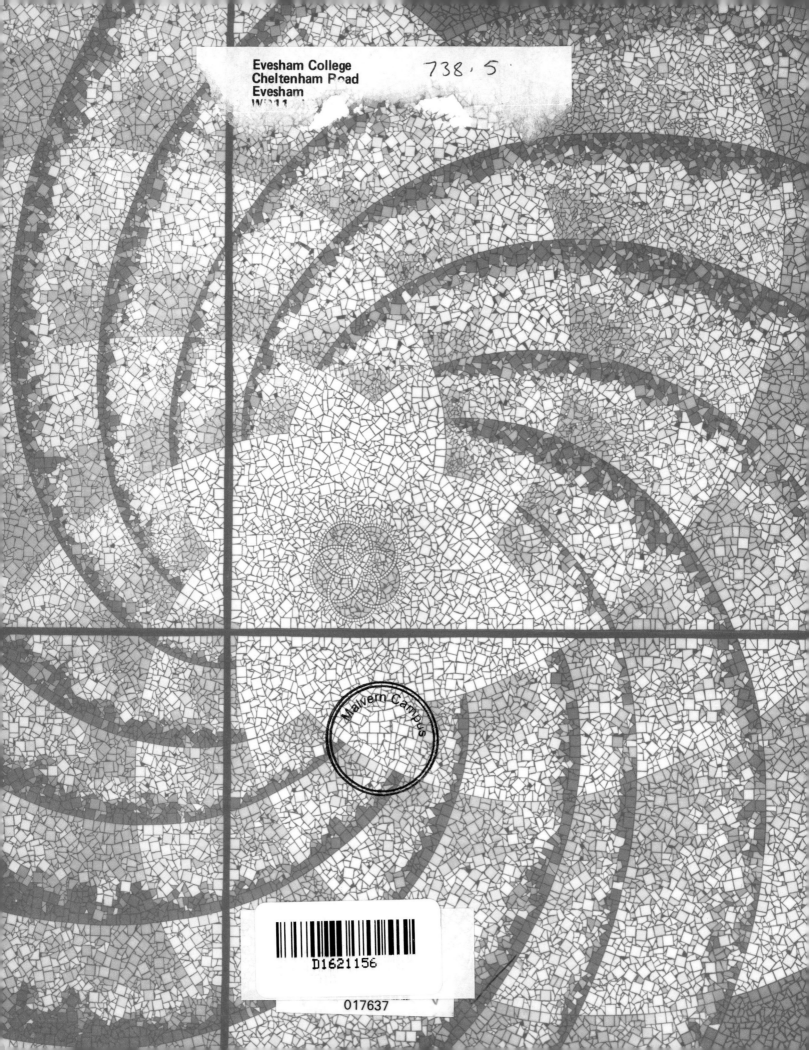

THE ART OF

MOSAIC DESIGN

A COLLECTION OF CONTEMPORARY ARTISTS

JoAnn Locktov and Leslie Plummer Clagett

First published in the United States of America by
Quarry Books, an imprint of
Rockport Publishers, Inc.
33 Commercial Street
Gloucester, Massachusetts 01930-5089
Telephone: (978) 282-9590
Fax: (978) 283-2742

Distributed to the book trade and art trade in the
United States by
North Light Books, an imprint of
F & W Publications
1507 Dana Avenue
Cincinnati, Ohio 45207
Telephone: (800) 289-0963

Other Distribution by
Rockport Publishers, Inc.
Gloucester, Massachusetts 01930-5089

ISBN 1-56496-420-5

10 9 8 7 6 5 4 3 2

Design: Minnie Cho Design

Cover Design: Sawyer Design Associates, Inc.

Front cover image: *Blue and Copper Gold*, by Lucio Orsoni
(see page 28 for full caption).

Back cover images: (clockwise from top) *Mexican Bean Pot*,
by Lynn Mattson (see page 111 for full caption); *Immigration 3:
Donato*, by Diana Maria Rossi (see page 33 for full caption);
Harmony's House, by Laura Bradley (see page 74 for full
caption); *Song of Summer (Self Portrait II)*, by Gary Stephens
(see page 56 for full caption).

Manufactured in China

This book was created to celebrate mosaics. It would have been impossible without the support of the mosaic artists who became my understanding partners in this adventure. In particular, I would like to thank Jane Muir for her international resourcefulness.

My thanks go to my agent Linda Allen, and from Rockport Publishers, Rosalie Grattaroti who had the unique vision to proceed, and Martha Wetherill for diligently completing the process.

I am grateful to Leslie Plummer Clagett who was able to put into words the passion I feel for this subject and Elena Marcheso Moreno who became involved with this project at its most fragile moment. I would also like to thank my friends Debby Fortune, for her belief in me, and Sandy Popovich, for always listening.

Finally, I thank my husband Steve Shapiro for his encouragement, and my children, Joseph and Eva, for their patience.

— JoAnn Locktov

TABLE OF CONTENTS

INTRODUCTION 6

GLASS MOSAICS 8

Erin Adams	10
Ellen Blakeley	14
Felice Nittolo	18
Lucio Orsoni	24
Diana Maria Rossi	30

CERAMIC MOSAICS 36

Joseph Blue Sky & Donna Webb	38
Gloria Kosco	44
Beryl Solla	50
Gary Stephens	54
Robert Stout & Stephanie Jurs	60

STONE MOSAICS 64

Linda Beaumont 66

Laura Bradley 72

Verdiano Marzi 78

MIXED MEDIA MOSAICS 84

Carlos Alves 86

Twyla Arthur 90

Candace Bahouth 94

Val Carroll 100

Lynn Mattson 106

Jane Muir 112

Lilli Ann Killen Rosenberg 116

Ilana Shafir 120

Isaiah Zagar 126

GALLERY OF ARTISTS 132

DIRECTORY OF ARTISTS 142

PHOTOGRAPHY CREDITS 144

Mosaic design is a fascinating art based on paradoxes that must be embraced. Among these are the pieces, multiple objects of simplicity fused into a singular, complex wholeness; the irregularity that springs from deliberation; and, more often than not, the creation that is wrought from destruction. Such paradoxes are put into context by the mosaicist when the principles of other visual arts are applied. By shaping *tesserae* like a sculptor, choosing colors like a painter, and weaving patterns like a fiber artist, the mosaicist presents his or her vision.

For the first time, in *The Art of Mosaic Design*, beautiful examples of the contemporary movement in mosaics are revealed; there are works presented here by mosaicists from around the world. Some of these artists have achieved great distinction, others quietly execute the works they are driven to create, but all will surely leave their imprint on the history of mosaic design as an art form.

That history is long. Some of civilization's earliest artistic expressions were rendered in mosaic as part of construction. Simple mosaics made of pebbles decorated pavements found in the People's Republic of China dating back more than two thousand years. By the fifth century B.C., the art of mosaic design was well established in Europe and the Mediterranean region, while figurative portrayals became increasingly sophisticated. Soon after that, the ability to cut rocks into small, regular units known as *tesserae* liberated the medium from its strictly functional role. This was a critical turning point for mosaics. Using these uniform pieces, stone murals could be applied to walls, ceilings, or other objects.

In addition, wide-spread production of glass allowed its regular incorporation into mosaics; its radiant, reflective qualities were accentuated against mortar, bringing new life to the art form. Following these improvements, ceramic *tesserae* were also included in mosaics. But it wasn't until the mid-twentieth century that the bridge between the three mosaic media would be anchored by mixed-media mosaic artists. In this final advancement, random objects are embedded into a composition, placing the emphasis on the parts rather than on the whole. Contemporary mosaics, which utilize all the media and concepts discussed above, have begun to garner much attention from the public.

Research for this book was done by word of mouth. There is no association for mosaic artists in the United States, no directory, gallery, or museum that specializes in this art form. Books on the subject offer "how-to" advice on assembling a mosaic, but none concentrate on the art. Few of the mosaic artists featured in this book have known more than one or two others who shared their passion, and for the most part they worked alone.

However, mosaic art has now started to become a part of modern society's collective consciousness. Just a few years ago, an American Express television advertisement featured Martha Stewart cutting up credit cards to "mosaic" her swimming pool. Hardly a home/design publication or upscale lifestyle magazine can be found without a sample of mosaic work. Retail home stores and catalogues offer accessories in the mosaic style, and a short ride along the New York subway presents an exhibition of the "new mosaics" along many station walls. Word has gotten out, and such popularity is sure to continue. The artists featured in this book, along with the rest of the world's mosaicists, will continue to create and share their passion, receiving ultimate critical praise and public recognition.

GLASS MOSAICS

Glass mosaics date from around the second century B.C., and became widespread by the fifth century, but it wasn't until the mid-fifteenth century when smalti manufacturers in Murano and Venice learned to precut small, regular pieces known as *tesserae*. These small units could be produced in a multitude of reflective colors that offered more diversity and potential than the options found with stone. While stone mosaics were limited somewhat by the size they could achieve with the tools available before they fractured, glass did not suffer this restriction. Even minute pieces of glass *tesserae* were possible to cut from the malleable glass threads blown from molten glass before it vitrifies.

Artists Felice Nittolo, Erin Adams, and Lucio Orsoni all work with the vivid smalti that characterizes historic glass mosaic artistry, yet their styles are anything but traditional. Rather than the church, geometric forms, magic carpets, and computer chips are the prevailing influences for their art, fashioned in the late 1990s. Although Diana Maria Rossi does include religion and the church in her colorful glass sculptures, it is more a reference to the struggle of an immigrant culture to assimilate than direct devotion. As for Ellen Blakeley, it can only be said that she has moved beyond the church to exalt the new religion of the streets. Tied together solely by their medium, this group of artists each offers their unique vision of life at the birth of a new millennium.

LUCIO ORSONI
Detail from
Black and Copper Gold

DIANA MARIA ROSSI
Detail from
Immigration 3: Donato

FELICE NITTOLO
Detail from
Sfera Rosa

ERIN ADAMS

Many of Erin Adams's glittering, glowing compositions of opaque, iridescent, and transparent glass are based on intricately patterned oriental rugs. As elements of interior design, these mosaic projects function just like their cloth counterparts—sometimes they act as area rugs, outlining a space; other times they dominate.

A childhood devoted to understanding the differences between good and bad art, under the hand of a very perceptive mother, eventually led Adams to pursue creative studies. While working on a master's degree from Pratt Institute, Adams focused on outsider art. After graduating, she opened a gallery of crossover art, then moved on to her own studio.

Detail from **Tapestry/Rug**
Radisson Empire Hotel, New York, New York

Detail from **Tapestry, Navajo Rug**

Erin Adams creates glass rugs patterned after kilim, Navajo, and oriental woven textiles. She designs each installation much like needlepoint: "While glass is as

TECHNIQUE

far away from fabric as possible, I try to make it seem malleable. A rug should look as though it's been walked on, so I shape the fringes to look as if disarranged, to have what we used to call 'toe hitches.' It is a visual joke, what I call 'vitreous humor.'" Her installations are also compatible with many types of flooring

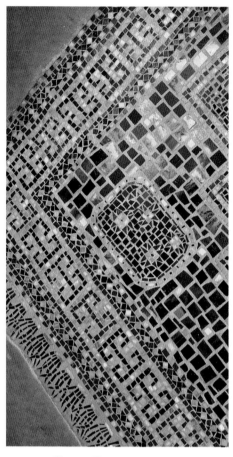

Detail from **Tapestry/Rug**
Cynthia Steffe Showroom, New York, New York

materials—they are typically surrounded by concrete, marble, or wood—and the gem-toned works catch and reflect all kinds of light.

The mosaicist's largest and most complex project to date is a 65,000-*tesserae* installation in a New York City hotel restaurant. Because the glass she

Detail from **Greek Key Table**

uses cannot be nipped into fragments smaller than .25 square inches (.5 square centimeters), this is a sizable project. Such elaborate projects are her passion. "I love the obsession of many, many parts making up a whole."

Detail from **Tapestry/Rug**, kitchen installation

Tapestry/Rug, kitchen installation
glass mosaic
14' x 5' (4.3 m x 1.5 m)

Bench (above)
glass mosaic
7' x 24" x 24" (2.1 meters x 60 cm x 60 cm)

Tapestry/Rug (below)
Radisson Empire Hotel, New York, New York
glass mosaic
16' x 6' (4.9 m x 1.8 m)

GALLERY

Tapestry/Rug
Cynthia Steffe Showroom, New York, New York
glass mosaic
10' x 6.5' (3 m x 2 m)

Greek Key Table
glass mosaic
7' x 5' (2.1 m x 1.5 m)

Tapestry, Navajo Rug
glass mosaic
36" x 20" (91 cm x 51 cm)

ELLEN BLAKELEY

Ellen Blakeley makes urban mosaics using the grit of city life. Forget marble, gemstones, gold and silver smalti, and even ceramics. This San Francisco artist's preferred medium is shattered safety glass salvaged from vandalized bus shelters and store windows. These found raw materials give Blakeley's mosaics a street-smart sensibility.

Blakeley's artistic career has evolved from printmaking and painting to ceramic sculpture and vessels to her current foray into glass mosaics. She studied ceramics under Ron Nagle at Mills College in Oakland, California, for four years, then opened a small tile design business that she ran from 1985 to 1992. Blakeley developed her special glass

mosaic technique in 1993, and since then she has found a ready market for a series of picture frames, tabletops, mirrors, and other household items. Her line of goods is being distributed in stores throughout the United States.

Collection of Mirrors
glass and collage, various sizes

Referring to her work as "recycled vandal-ism," the artist gives glass shards center stage in her projects. She discovered her inventive shattered glass technique about

TECHNIQUE

five years ago, treating broken tempered glass as her *tesserae*. Rather than obliter-ating the surface below, the glass opens it up as another dimension within each artwork where colors and patterns sparkle.

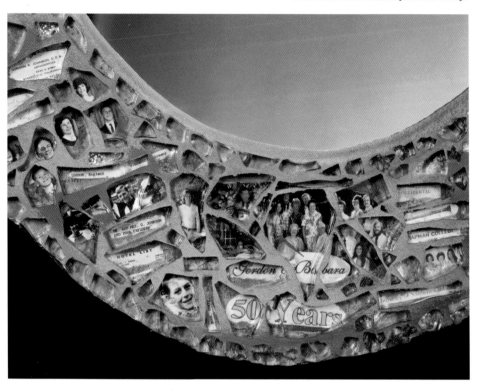

Fragments are the basic mosaic building blocks, but they also act as unobtrusive lenses to view collage images that lie beneath them. Bits of patterned paper, colored foil, drawings, photographs, and printed text are used

to create different effects. Because thick pieces of glass often contain webs of internal fractures, the compositions have extraordinary refractive qualities. "The

information that goes under the glass, along with the pureness of the glass itself, keeps me endlessly intrigued with the play between surface and depth," she says.

Details from **Rebar Console Table** (above and right)

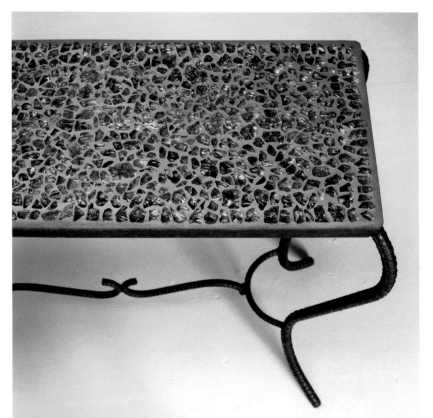

15

Oval Mirror
glass and collage
36" x 27" x 1" (91 cm x 69 cm x 3 cm)

Octagon Mirror
glass and collage
12" x 8" (30 cm x 20 cm)

Men, Women, and Money
glass and collage
9" x 17" x 1" (23 cm x 43 cm x 3 cm)

Rebar Console Table
glass and collage
3.3' x 3.8' (1 meter x 1.1 meters)

River under the Glass
glass and collage
18" x 10" x 1" (46 cm x 25 cm x 3 cm)

FELICE NITTOLO

Mosaic artist and sculptor of wide renown, Felice Nittolo maintains his studio in Ravenna, Italy, considered by many to be the classic source of traditional mosaics since the fifth and sixth centuries. However, Nittolo is focused on breaking the rules and creating a new tradition.

Nittolo's provocative sculptures are rendered as pyramids, cones, spheres, totems, and pillars. These innovative volumes are vibrantly glazed in Byzantine mosaic—the artist's trademark—highlighting shapes, materials, and colors. His unique viewpoint offers geometric speculation, a visual perception of space executed in terms of light and shadow.

He has taught mosaic art since 1982 at the Istituto Statale d'Arte in Ravenna, where he imparts his perspective on art. "We must transmit *our* time. Today we have to react to recent academic tradition in order to fit in with the needs of a society that has been changing at a faster and faster pace. We have to force a radical renewal in the very concept of art."

Detail from **Always Mosaic**

New ideas are few and far between in the contemporary art world, according to Felice Nittolo. "Mosaic has aesthetic value of great severity and innovation;

TECHNIQUE

the tesserae—each one of them—are unique. They cannot be replicated," says Nittolo.

True to this belief, the artist often manipulates the interstices between the tesserae in his pieces, sometimes exaggerating empty spaces so that the smalti suggests thin strands of beads lying across an expanse of sand. In other instances, he sets them together so tightly that they appear to be woven like fabric.

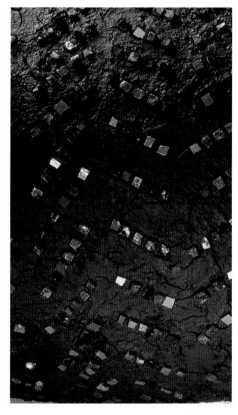

Detail from **Coperton**

These spatial explorations often go a step further and assume three dimensions; by using cardboard, plastic materials, or lightweight acrylic resins for the tile

armature, Nittolo is able to initiate yet another departure from conventional mosaic designs, while making his art very much of his own era. In his own words, "the mosaic *tessera* can do away with the present crisis of ideas since it

Detail from **Baco da Seta**

is . . . a tradition anew. Mosaic has aesthetic and artistic values of great severity and innovation; the *tesserae* are, each one of them, unique."

Detail from **Always Mosaic**

Always Mosaic
glass mosaic and glass
29" x 19" (73 cm x 48 cm)

Baco da Seta
glass mosaic and marble
17" x 7" x 7" (45 cm x 18 cm x 18 cm)

GALLERY

Coperton (below)
glass mosaic, gold, marble, and tar
19" x 16" x 10" (48 cm x 44 cm x 26 cm)

Omino (above)
glass mosaic, glass, marble, and mirror
35" x 23" diameter (89 cm x 57 cm diameter)

Bozzolo
glass mosaic, marble, and metal
4.8' x 24" x 24" (1.4 m x 60 cm x 60 cm)

Sella d'Argento
miope, silver, aluminum, and glass
12" x 6" x 5" (30 cm x 15 cm x 13 cm)

Cono Blu
glass mosaic, lead, and ceramic
7" diameter x 15" (18 cm diameter x 37 cm)

Biciclo con Sella (above)
miope, silver, aluminum, glass, and velocipede

Sfera Rosa
glass mosaic
11" diameter (28 cm diameter)

Installazione
glass mosaic, wood, and steel
6.5' x 3.3' x 20" (2 m x 1 m x 50 cm)

Sfera Nera
glass mosaic, marble, and gold
11" diameter (28 cm diameter)

Il Mondo
glass mosaic, marble, yellow terra cotta, and gold
34" diameter (85 cm diameter)

Cono Nero
glass mosaic, marble, coal, and lava
7" diameter x 15" (18 cm diameter x 37 cm)

LUCIO ORSONI

Born in 1939, Venice artist Lucio Orsoni studied art in Venice, presented his works at numerous exhibitions, and then concentrated strictly on mosaics for the Angelo Orsoni family factory. For more than thirty years, in addition to his creative work, Orsoni has been deeply involved in the supply side of art. He has been producing *smalti e ori per mosaico* for the family business, which is one of the few remaining smalti manufacturers in the world.

With their saturated colors and deliberate, skillful shading, Orsoni's smalti mosaics echo the techniques and objectives of classical artistic precedent. His work then takes leave of that figurative tradition, with its exacting, ordered geometry. His compositions are similar to labyrinth tracings, and have been likened in appearance to computer microchips.

Detail from **Oro Ramino**

Among the most visually engaging of Orsoni's monochromatic studies are his gold-tinted pieces. The artist pairs black tesserae with a particular hue of gold—

TECHNIQUE

blue gold, grey gold, violet gold, or white gold—in a basic checkerboard pattern to create fields of graduated color that are literally vibrant. As the shapes formed by the smalti optically recede into, and grow out of, the plane of the image, a hypnotic visual effect takes place. A few of these installations

Detail from **As a Compliment to Constable**

are large; one piece, *Palazzo Ferro Fini*, measures 5.3 feet by 7.8 feet (1.6 meters by 2.4 meters) and was constructed in sections.

Disturbed by the decline of mosaic artistry over the centuries, Orsoni found little inspiration from most historical works. He now sees that the rebirth of

Detail from **Bianco E Oro**

mosaics as a fine art has come about at last, and he is grateful to those artists who have begun to create them again: ". . . thanks to the works of those artists who have begun again, and who continue, to think mosaic."

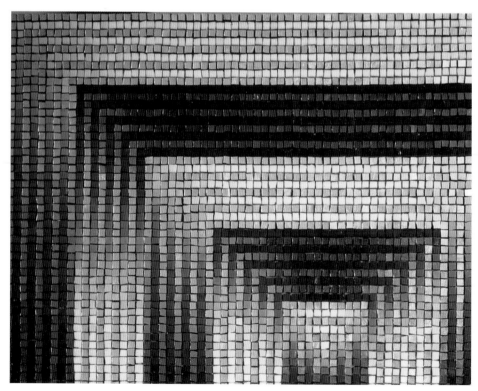

Detail from **Blue and Copper Gold**

As a Compliment to Constable
Venetian glass smalti
4' x 4' (1.2 m x 1.2 m)

Mane Nobiscum Domine Quia Vesperascit,
3 panels
Venetian glass smalti
4' x 4' (1.2 m x 1.2 m) each

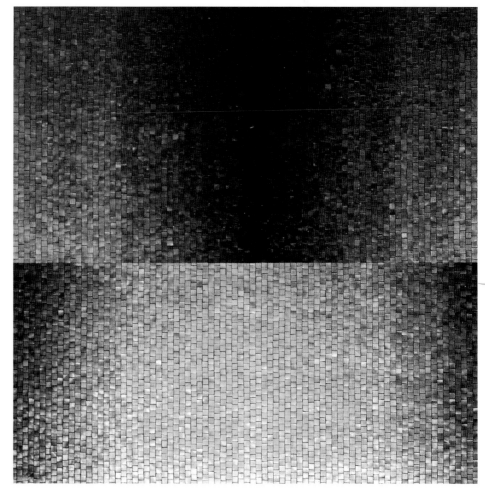

Oro Ramino
Venetian glass smalti
3.3' x 3.3' (1 m x 1 m)

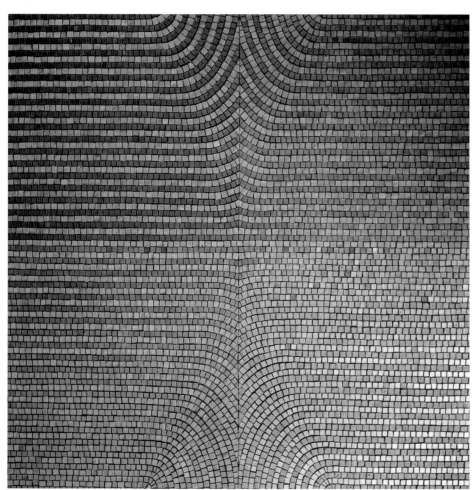

Bianco E Oro
35th Biennale 1970
Venetian glass smalti
3.3' x 3.3' (1 m x 1 m)

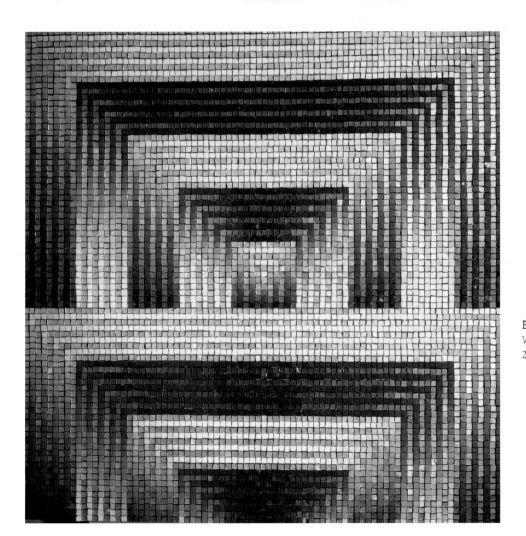

Blue and Copper Gold
Venetian glass smalti
20" x 20" (50 cm x 50 cm)

Black and Copper Gold
Venetian glass smalti
35" x 35" (89 cm x 89 cm)

Black and White Gold
Venetian glass smalti
3.6' x 3.6' (1.1 m x 1.1 m)

GALLERY

Black, Light Blue, and Violet Gold
Venetian glass smalti
4.3' x 4.3' (1.3 m x 1.3 m)

Bronze Gold
Venetian glass smalti
3.3' x 3.3' (1 m x 1 m)

Black and Blue Gold
Venetian glass smalti
4.5' x 4.5' (1.4 m x 1.4 m)

DIANA MARIA ROSSI

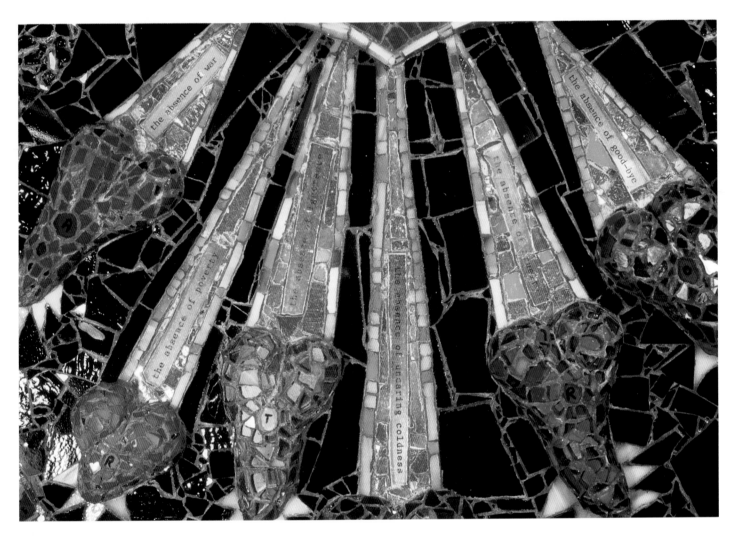

Diana Maria Rossi's glass mosaics create an emotional impact rarely experienced in this medium due to the social content of her work. As she explores thought-provoking themes such as the pain and dislocation of immigrants and home and homelessness, she creates vivid, iconographic images. For the last decade, Rossi has been making mosaics that unite her formal training in printmaking at the San Francisco Art Institute with her affinity for vivid colors and Italian-Polish-American heritage.

Her fascination with many of her subjects is likely due to the environment in which she was raised—Catholic churches and Italian-American living rooms. "Many of my sensibilities were cultivated in these places—ornate sanctuaries of rococo embellishment," she says. Quite a few of her mosaic portraits have been singled out for the substance they give to all kinds of faces, from peasant to prom queen.

Detail from **A Rebuttal for My Critics (with Aunt Bea Watching)**

Portraits, hearts, and landscapes are the basic images Diana Maria Rossi utilizes, and her social consciousness and meaningful themes are expressed through mosaics.

TECHNIQUE

Rossi has developed a technique that supports her vision. In her direct method of mosaic design, the *tesserae* are laid into mortar and then grouted, a process that joins glass chips of various thicknesses together into a highly faceted, reflective surface. "This technique allows

Detail from **Immigration 3: Donato**

me to pull out all the stops," states the artist, "to revel in the glittery, jewel-like nature of glass, to explore my idea of beauty. By working in this manner, I hope to show respect for the aesthetic qualities which comprise my cultural heritage." Of her portraits, Rossi says, "I want to make explicit the beauty in every face, the saint in each of us." She has also made hundreds of mosaic hearts in an attempt to give substance to a symbol that is often trivialized and cast aside as a cliché.

Details from **For My Grandparents: Assunta, Donata, Eva, and Jacob**

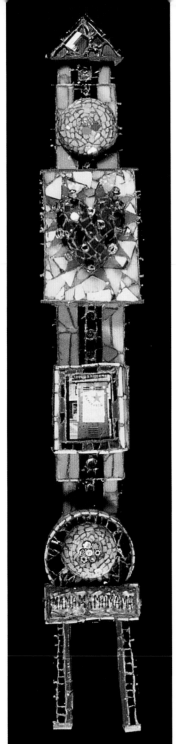

Modern Motherhood
glass mosaic on wood with nails and photographs
2.5" x 17" x 1.5" (6 cm x 43 cm x 4 cm)

**A Rebuttal for My Critics
(with Aunt Bea Watching)**
glass mosaic on wood
15.5" x 16.75" x .75" (39 cm x 42 cm x 2 cm)

For My Grandparents: Assunta, Donata, Eva, and Jacob
glass mosaic on wood with photographs
24" x 5.5" x .75" (60 cm x 14 cm x 2 cm)

GALLERY

Immigration 3: Donato
glass mosaic on wood with photograph
4.25" x 5.5" x 1.5" (10 cm x 14 cm x 4 cm)

Angela di Cortile Cascino
glass mosaic on wood
12" x 12.75" x .75" (30 cm x 31 cm x 2 cm)

To Be Female and Free
glass mosaic on wood
4.25" x 3.75" x 1.5" (10 cm x 9 cm x 4 cm)

Flavia
glass mosaic on wood
4.75" x 7.5" x .75" (12 cm x 19 cm x 2 cm)

Lost Between the Present and the Past Imagining the Future
glass mosaic on wood with paint
7" x 9" x 5" (18 cm x 23 cm x 13 cm)

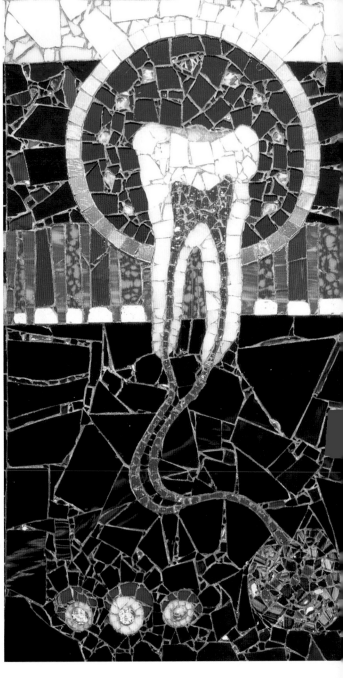

Destiny Takes Us to Strange Places (for Rita)
glass mosaic on wood
10.5" x 18" x .75" (27 cm x 46 cm x 2 cm)

Delicious Bodies
glass mosaic on wood
4.75" x 5.75" x 1" (12 cm x 14 cm x 3 cm)

Truth
glass mosaic on wood
5.25" x 6" x 1.5" (13 cm x 15 cm x 4 cm)

Marcella
glass mosaic on wood
5.5" x 7" x .75" (14 cm x 18 cm x 2 cm)

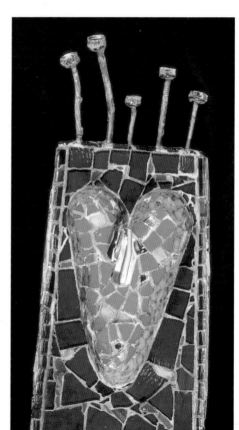

It's a Hard Full Life
glass mosaic on wood
with nails
3.5" x 6" x 1.5"
(9 cm x 15 cm x 4 cm)

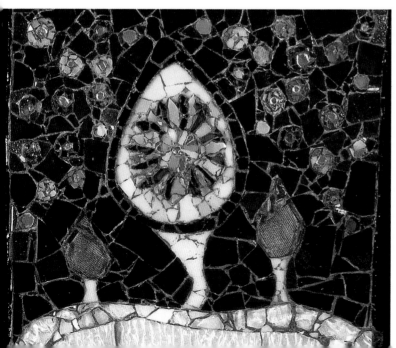

Starry Night (Thanks Vincent)
glass mosaic on wood
5.5" x 5.5" x .75" (14 cm x 14 cm x 2 cm)

The core of the turn-of-the-century Art Nouveau movement was a passion for 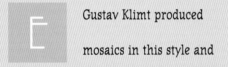 decorative motifs; flowing patterns and stylized forms were to be found in architecture and the arts throughout Europe. Austrian painter 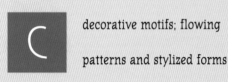 Gustav Klimt produced mosaics in this style and took the medium to a new level through his murals. Architect/artist Antonio Gaudi, who had sheathed many of his fanciful structures in glazed ceramics, can also be credited for validating the medium.

 Contemporaries, both Klimt and Gaudi set the stage for experiments in tactility and innovations in materials that the artists featured here all continue today.

Robert Stout and Stephanie Jurs, Joseph Blue Sky and Donna Webb, Gloria Kosco, Beryl Solla, and Gary Stephens have moved beyond the Art Nouveau style, yet their patterns are often stylized in flowing form. While their works are quite varied, these artists represent the latest thinking in ceramic mosaics. Like Gaudi, their works transcend the two-dimensionality of historic mosaics and pave the way for cutting-edge ventures into tactility.

LORIA KOSCO
tail from
ivate Bathroom Installation

ROBERT STOUT AND STEPHANIE JURS
Detail from
The Pathway I

BERYL SOLLA
Detail from
Home of the Brave II, small fountain

The art of Joseph Blue Sky and Donna Webb deals with the relationship of architecture to figures and other objects and the way they all combine to tell a story without words. Partners, they work together as one—each contributes their disparate talents to create a unified whole. Blue Sky is the model crafter and carpenter, while Webb brings a lively sense of color and a sure hand at the potter's wheel and kiln. Thus, their collaboration becomes synergistic.

In their installation for the University of Akron School of Art, a revealing collection of figures stylized in various ceramic arts applications emerges from the picture's plane. Blue Sky and Webb incorporate ancient pottery forms, classical statuary, formal portrait busts, and modern figurative sculpture into the mural. These elements are modeled in extreme relief and posed next to a towering kiln in this engrossing chronicle of the eras and styles of art history.

Detail from **King Triton and the Little Mermaid**, mural in collaboration with Group See

Bringing a well-rounded aesthetic to their mosaic projects, Joseph Blue Sky and Donna Webb claim, "We are not minimalists but more like maximalists,

TECHNIQUE

in that color, sculptural form, composition, function, and storytelling contribute meaning to our work."

The pair strives to equally develop a pictorial sense as well as a rich and varied surface treatment—narrative and dimension are among their prime concerns. "We like to explore the middle ground between painting and sculpture that tile occupies," they explain.

Detail from **Magic Fountain**

Historically, tile integrates easily with architecture. "It achieves a tactile materiality not possible with canvas painting,

yet it also allows exploration of color and composition. This combination suits our talents and our special kind of storytelling"—much, they feel, like Gaudi, Tiffany, and Michelangelo did before them in decorating walls, ceilings, and floors of churches and

Detail from **Ceramic Mural**

public buildings. "In doing our work we take the roles of 'The Makers.' These characters are from a story we wrote about an old man and an old woman who are constantly renewing the world . . . . We believe that making art is a way of making ourselves and our world, and of defining our culture for future generations."

Detail from **Four Seasons Floor**

Details from **Four Seasons Floor**
Central Ohio Psychiatric Hospital
ceramic with wood sculpture by Charlotte Lees

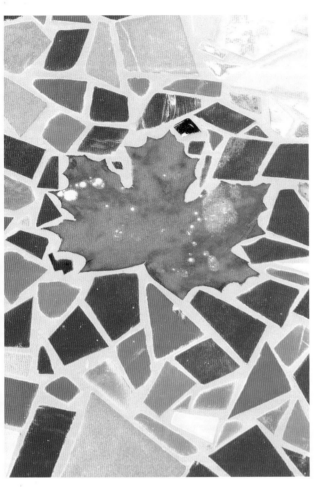

King Triton and the Little Mermaid,
mural in collaboration with Group See
(above) *Children's Hospital, Akron, Ohio*
ceramic
24' x 8' (7.3 m x 2.4 m)

Details from **Four Seasons Floor**
(left and above left)
Central Ohio Psychiatric Hospital

Details from **Magic Fountain**
*The Tree House, a children's room at
the Metro Health Center, Cleveland, Ohio*
ceramic

Ceramic Mural
School of Art, University of Akron, Ohio
ceramic
12' x 12' (3.7 m x 3.7 m)

Details from **Ceramic Mural**
(above and left)
School of Art, University of Akron, Ohio
ceramic

GLORIA KOSCO

Gloria Kosco holds degrees in ceramics from the Rhode Island School of Design and the School for American Crafts at the Rochester Institute of Technology. For nine years, she worked with Mimi Strang under the umbrella of Decoratta Ornamental Terra Cotta, a collaborative artists' studio where the two investigated the relationships between ornament and architecture, often within the rigorous confines of municipal Percent-for-Art competitions and commissions. Now on her own, Kosco explores the nature of time, a favorite theme of her public works.

Although most of the visual vocabulary that appears in her public installations is re-examined in her fine arts pieces, the latter group tells a more personal story. Densely tiled with diminutive images of stars, flames, water, and wheels—sometimes cast as compasses or other forms that function as allegories for time—Kosco creates art with primitive overtones and universal appeal.

Detail from **Undercurrents**

In constructing her site-specific sundials, Gloria Kosco first surveys the location, observing the interaction of light and landscape elements. Then she sets the

TECHNIQUE

center point of the circle and determines the true north heading. Generally, the artist excavates a dozen shallow forms or cavities around the circle's perimeter, making an adobe mixture from the earth.

With this mud, she builds the sundial's central gnomon and its four cardinal points. Placing the adobe mixture back into the shallow cavities, Kosco then inlays colorful bits of glazed terra cotta into the surface to complete the project. The result is twelve plaques—the adobe mixture with inlaid pieces of terra cotta—that punctuate the circle. In each of these works, the earth serves triple duty—form, molded material, and fired material—infusing symbolic and structural strength into her sundials.

"My imagery parallels my interests," says Kosco. "I am influenced by things I like, things I read about, recollections of my past,

Detail from **Private Bathroom Installation**

questionable occurrences, perplexing events, things that impress me, and things I know."

Detail from **Relative Degree of Plentifulness**

Voyage from the Temporal, III
ceramic and masonry
5.3' x 35" x 3" (1.6 m x 89 cm x 8 cm)

Undercurrents
ceramic and masonry
5.3' x 33" x 3"
(1.6 m x 84 cm x 8 cm)

**Private Bathroom Installation, a
collaboration with Mimi Strang**
ceramic, slate, and masonry

**Private Kitchen Floor Installation,
a collaboration with Mimi Strang**
ceramic, slate, and masonry

Relative Degree of Plentifulness, pedestal planter,
a collaboration with Mimi Strang
ceramic and masonry, thrown and hand-built
3.5' x 16" x 16" (1.1 m x 41 cm x 41 cm)

Time IV, Fireplace 2
(above right, detail at right)
ceramic and masonry
4.8' x 5.3' x 16" (1.4 m x 1.6 m x 41 cm)
fireplace doors, cast iron and tempered glass
28" x 36" x 1" (71 cm x 91 cm x 3 cm)

Sundial '92, a collaboration with Mimi Strang
(below, details at right)
Cedar Beach Park, Allentown, Pennsylvania
ceramic and masonry, 35' diameter (10.7 m diameter)
central gnomon, 6' high (1.8 m high), surrounded by
an inner ring of spherical time markers
and an outer ring of twelve 36" (91 cm) plaques

Penland Sundial, a collaboration with Mimi Strang and 20 students
(above, details at left)
Penland School of Crafts, Penland, North Carolina
terra cotta clay and modified concrete
40" diameter (12.2 m diameter)
arch-shaped time markers, 12" x 5" (30 cm x 13 cm) each

The idea that art should reflect the culture in which it is made and the people who view it aptly describes the aesthetic principle of mosaic artist Beryl Solla, more so than the prevailing view that art is a personal expression of the individual. Filled with metaphors and inspiration meant for those who will be regularly exposed to it, her site-specific works offer promise and hope.

Yet, in a medium that is difficult to imbue with personality, Solla has achieved an artistic identity that is instantly recognizable. Embedded in her two-dimensional murals are figures—tile silhouettes with charmingly clumsy and child-like edges—in solid planes of color, unencumbered by detail or texture. A Pop Art palette of striking shades, anchored by muted tones of turquoise,

primary red and yellow, lavender, and mossy green, withstands the relentless Florida sunshine and gives a nod to the varied hues of the area's Art Deco architecture. For Solla, mosaic is metaphor: broken tile that unites communities and mends shattered lives.

Detail from **Home of the Brave II**

"I believe that public art paid for by the government should reflect the needs and interests of the community using the space. If possible, I try to involve the

TECHNIQUE

local group in the piece by incorporating their history in some conceptual way or by inviting them to make tiles with me," says Beryl Solla.

For a Florida alcohol and drug recovery center, Solla designed, fabricated, and installed a work in keeping with her philosophy. Executed in two parts, *Home of the Brave* is indeed inspirational.

Embracing the entrance of an otherwise stark white stucco building is a ground-level mural of symbolism—healing hearts, hands, and houses shaded by palm trees

Detail from **Home of the Brave II, small fountain**

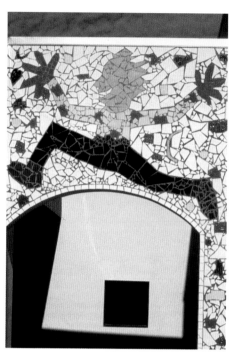

Detail from **Jump!**

are set against white and black backgrounds. These same motifs are repeated on a tiled patio and fountain in back.

At the Children's Creative Center, a daycare center and school in Miami, Solla's mosaics convey growth. Two panels featuring jumping children flank its entry, while the confetti-like pattern of the ceramics overflows onto the surrounding sidewalk.

Detail from **Me and My Tropical-Fruit-Flavored Shadow**

BERYL SOLLA

Top Ten Things
St. Agnes Rainbow Village Day Care Center,
Miami, Florida
ceramic tile
250 square feet (75 square meters)

Jump!
Florida International University
ceramic tile
180 square feet (54 square meters)

Me and My Tropical-Fruit-Flavored Shadow, 2 panels
Carol Donaldson Day Care Center, Miami, Florida
ceramic tile
8' x 8' (2.4 m x 2.4 m) each

Working
Metro-Dade Building, Miami, Florida
ceramic tile
8' x 6' (2.4 m x 1.8 m)

Home of the Brave II, small fountain
Booher Addiction and Recovery Center,
Coral Springs, Florida, ceramic tile
450 square feet (45 square meters)

GARY STEPHENS

Northern California artist Gary Stephens creates life-affirming and truly unique mosaic sculptures. Using vividly colored shards of pottery and tile, he celebrates the pleasures of nature and its abundance through the colorful tropical fruit, fish, and birds that he renders within the context of stylized self-portraits. Central to much of Stephens's work are musical instruments and birds in song—highlighting an affinity for music, particularly in happy moments.

Stephens first trained as a painter, then turned to pottery and jewelry because he was fascinated with the concept of "making things." But it was mosaic sculpture that finally let him capture in three dimensions and vibrant colors the joy that he sees in everyday occurrences. His mosaics depict mermen, angels, and other mythological figures, all busy paying homage to nature's cycles and enjoying the vitality around them. Combining patterned dishware, figurines, and brilliant glazes, Stephens pieces together playful and inspiring works.

Detail from **Song of Summer (Self-Portrait II)**

"Bright colors are joyful and uplifting. I use them to counter the dark side of art often fostered by the art school culture—to be serious, analytical, critical, and

TECHNIQUE

portray unhappy emotions. Instead, my idea is to offer a happy and whimsical presentation of life," says Gary Stephens. Raised in an Arizona border town, he was exposed frequently to the direct simplicity of Mexican folk art, which Stephens says has helped shape his style.

Rather than strictly embracing traditional mosaic working methods,

Detail from **Angel of Vision**

Stephens developed his own technique of incising *faux tesserae* into the ceramic to complete a composition. His work is greatly influenced by the shiny, busy

quality of Thai mosaic artists that he studied on his travels, as well as by the works of Rousseau, Chagall, and Matisse. Whether he is combing through boxes of dishes at yard sales or buying tea bowls by the dozen in

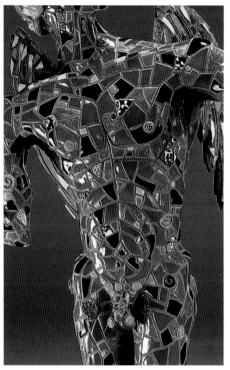

Detail from **Bobbing for Apples**

San Francisco's Chinatown, Stephens looks constantly for the perfect pattern—flowers to dot a merman's cheekbones, or scrolls and swirls for an angel's hair.

Detail from **Fish Worship**

Song of Summer (Self-Portrait II)
mosaic on wood
40" x 31" x 3" (102 cm x 79 cm x 8 cm)

Bobbing for Apples
mosaic and low-fire ceramic
30" x 18" x 10"
(76 cm x 46 cm x 25 cm)

Angel of Vision
mosaic and found objects on wood
24" x 17" x 4" (60 cm x 43 cm x 10 cm)

Fish Worship
mosaic and low-fire ceramic on wood
48" x 30" x 5" (122 cm x 76 cm x 13 cm)

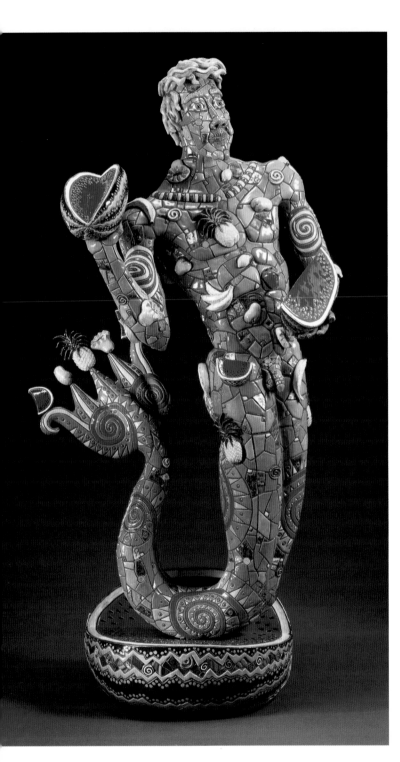

Watermelon Merman
mosaic, high-fire ceramic, low-fire glaze
36" x 19" x 12" (91 cm x 48 cm x 30 cm)

Frog Fountain with Halo of Bugs
mosaic and high-fire ceramic
8' x 4' x 4' (2.4 m x 1.2 m x 1.2 m)

Earth Angel Sings the Wildlife Blues
mosaic on wood
40" x 34" x 5" (102 cm x 86 cm x 13 cm)

Song of Summer (Self-Portrait I)
mosaic and low-fire ceramic
28" x 20" x 5" (71 cm x 51 cm x 13 cm)

In their collaboration as Twin Dolphin Mosaics, Robert Stout and Stephanie Jurs expand the historic traditions of Roman and Byzantine mosaics through modern science and mathematics. Their work draws its inspiration from scientific imagery and patterns.

Their design for a walkway at the Albuquerque Museum's sculpture garden comprises two parts. First there are two sets of logarithmic spirals, appearing somewhat like the bottom of an open pine cone. The second element is a spouting, spring-like image based on a computer-generated illustration of one of the principles of fluid mechanics.

Stout has a background in drawing and painting; Jurs has a background in graphic design and crafts. Together they have completed arts projects in Alaska, California, and New Mexico.

These two dedicated artists recently relocated to Ravenna, Italy, to study Classical and Byzantine mosaic techniques, a historical and powerful mosaic tradition that will enable them to pursue their goal of creating mosaics with twentieth-century themes.

Details from
Curved Surface, mosaic entryway

Robert Stout finds that mosaics have "potential residing primarily in contemporary investigations of nature." The bounds of scientific observation have

TECHNIQUE

been pushed to extremes, and he feels "a responsibility as an artist to use this imagery, along with color, intuition, and emotion, to create pieces that describe the world in a different context."

Detail from **The Pathway I**

Speaking of the scientific patterns underlying the formation of the spirals in the Albuquerque Museum walkway, Stout observes, "I value the idea that out of an original chaotic state there emerge beautiful, orderly patterns." The lace-like quality of the project owes its delicacy to the thinness of its grout lines and small *tesserae*.

In future works, Twin Dolphin Mosaics will expand on the theme of nature seen through the lenses of scientific discipline. "We find these images compelling and beautiful," they say, for they believe these concepts are perfectly suited for the complicated medium of mosaics.

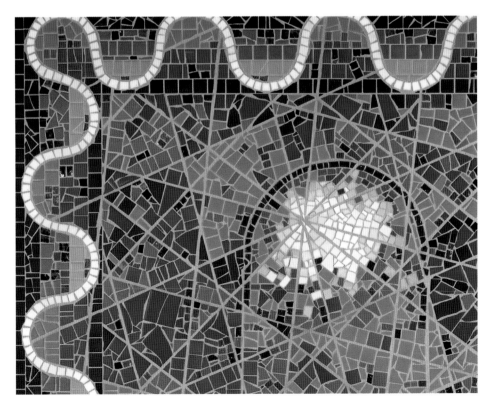

Detail from **Vita Nuova**

Curved Surface, mosaic entryway
Donelly Library, Highlands University,
Las Vegas, New Mexico
Italian- and Byzantine-style glass smalti
and Italian ceramic tile
930 square feet (279 square meters)

Vita Nuova
solid body porcelain and glass smalti
3.7' x 3.7' (1.1 m x 1.1 m)

Detail from
Curved Surface, mosaic entryway

GALLERY

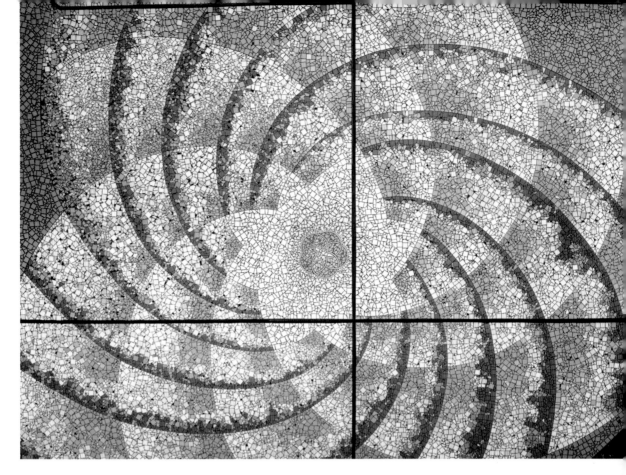

The Pathway I
Albuquerque Museum, New Mexico
tile mosaic
35' x 30' (10.7 m x 9.1 m)

The Pathway II
Albuquerque Museum, New Mexico
tile mosaic
35' x 35' (10.7 m x 10.7 m)

STONE MOSAICS

The very nature of stone mosaics connects them to the natural world and man's 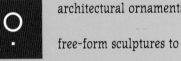 ancient past. Yet, rather than being primitive, contemporary stone mosaic design is a highly evolved and sophisticated art form. Stone, rock, and rubble carefully arranged into compositions can create a look that appears to be random.

With the development of more precise cutting tools between the fifth and fifteenth centuries, stones were more easily cut into small, lightweight, uniform pieces known as *tesserae*. From that point, mosaics entered the realm of the decorative and began to appear as applications on walls and ceilings. Today they are seen in these forms and many others, from large-scale architectural ornaments to free-form sculptures to coverings for household objects.

While their individual styles diverge dramatically, stone mosaic artists Linda Beaumont, Laura Bradley, and Verdiano Marzi share some common ground. All take the viewer on a journey, although the destinations are not similar.

Beaumont's works carry the individual on a spiritual pilgrimage beyond themselves; Bradley's murals are likely to create more personal introspection; and Marzi's jagged silhouettes and rough-hewn stone take you to the natural world. The intentional rustication of Bradley's stone works and Marzi's smaller works contrast with the polished softness of Beaumont's, yet all have pieces that feature stone in a raw state suggestive of an unseen creative hand.

RDIANO MARZI
ail from
erior Wall Mosaic

LAURA BRADLEY
Detail from
Apocalypse

LINDA BEAUMONT
Detail from
Full Circle

LINDA BEAUMONT

For more than seventeen years, Seattle artist Linda Beaumont has been working in mosaics, piecing together her creations stone by stone. Considering herself a "public artist," Beaumont has a large body of work that includes paintings, traditional ceramic mosaics, and her present endeavors in stone and *terrazzo*.

Beaumont is best known for her compositions of found objects and earthy materials that at first seem simple but upon closer inspection prove to be quite complex. The surfaces of her mosaics have a generous spirit to them that invites the mind to slow down and the hand to touch. From fountains to pavements, floors, and columns, Beaumont's stone mosaics are site-specific, and her works grace both public and private facilities throughout the city of Seattle. George Chacona, a Seattle artist, developed a method for etching marble with imagery and shared his time and artistic energy with Linda during the fabrication of the Bailey Boushay Entryway and of "Full Circle."

Details from **Water for Fire**, **Bailey Boushay, entry vestibule** (above and left)

Ornate, tiled temples and cobblestone paths encountered on journeys abroad have all etched their imprint on Linda Beaumont. The work of Gaudi, the temples

TECHNIQUE

of Thailand, and the pathways of Portugal are the underlying sources of her inspiration, but Beaumont's interpretations of the projects she undertakes are purely her own.

At one of Seattle's residential care facilities for persons with AIDS, Beaumont designed and installed two stone mosaics

Details from **Bailey Boushay, donor recognition pillar** (above and left)

intended more for the residents than for visitors. The building is the last environment many of them will witness, she says. "The responsibility to make an entry that could touch people was too great. I needed clues, and touch was my first." She used shards of onyx and marble in sandy, earthy tones to create a gentle yet logical transitional space.

Then she embellished the stone with added imagery by etching the marble with ancient symbols such as feet walking on water and in fire, which she relates to the lives of people living with AIDS.

Water for Fire, Bailey Boushay, entry vestibule
AIDS Hospice
onyx and stone mosaic, embedded with mementos and etched marble
10' x 10' x 15' (3 m x 3 m x 4.6 m)

Bailey Boushay, donor recognition pillar
(above, detail at left) *AIDS Hospice*
etched marble, found objects, and mementos
3' x 3' x 3' x 10' (.9 m x .9 m x .9 m x 3 m)

Step On No Pets
Animal Control Center
ceramic mosaic
10' x 15' x 8" (3 m x 4.6 m x 20 cm)

Full Circle

Harbor View Hospital
terrazzo and photo images of ancient Roman
mosaics etched into travertine and brass
1,800 square feet (540 square meters)

GALLERY

Details from **Sturgis Church, private altar**
stone and ceramic mosaic and found objects

LAURA BRADLEY

Having worked in almost every art form, Laura Bradley is also trained in some construction trades, including masonry. Her vibrant artistic stone expressions are the result of applying her training in one medium to another medium. Bradley develops ideas in collage and watercolor alongside her mosaics, and enjoys the particular constraints of working on an intimate scale: "I find the most freedom in ideas of limited space—the push and pull of a collage or the illusion of a window in watercolor may appear again as a copper door with small mosaic columns on either side."

Portals are a recurring theme throughout her work, representing communication that begins with an entry and continues with the journey through each piece. She uses portals to blend classical architecture and ornaments within her assemblages, regardless of the materials. This artistic emphasis can be seen in her commissions for the New York City Transit Authority where she has not only designed a series of subway station mosaics, but has also created a complete program of railings, gates, and grillwork.

Details from **Harmony's House**
(above and opposite)

The commitment to creating mosaics that Laura Bradley demonstrates extends far beyond her studio. Personally collecting stones to cut by hand into tesserae helps

TECHNIQUE

to immerse Bradley in her art. "I may be in the woods all day where I know there are traces of an old riverbed layered beneath the topsoil. Often, a single small stone, uncut in my hand, helps an image to rise spontaneously," she says.

She turns such images into the mosaic portals for which she is famous. Her inventive palette of materials

Detail from **Going Home**

includes marble and stone, and she often incorporates copper, silver, bronze, steel, mica, aluminum, and brass into her

pieces. Looking through the pictorial doorways she frames inspires a certain reverie. "Stones seem to have the quality of speaking about time—forever remembering and constantly hoping,"

Detail from **The Open Gate**

reflects Bradley. Some of her panels cluster around openings, while others exhibit a single glimpse of another time and place.

Silver Doorway
hand-cut marble mosaic, bronze,
fossil, stone, brass, silver, and ceramic
4.7' x 25" x 3" (1.4 m x 64 cm x 8 cm)

Harmony's House
hand-cut marble mosaic, stone, copper,
ceramic, and bronze
4.3' x 20" x 4" (1.3 m x 51 cm x 10 cm)

Going Home
hand-cut marble mosaic, stone,
bronze, brass, and ceramic
4' x 22" x 3" (1.2 m x 56 cm x 8 cm)

The Open Gate
hand-cut marble mosaic,
brass, and ceramic
27" x 26" x 2" (68 cm x 66 cm x 5 cm)

Annunziation I
hand-cut marble mosaic wall
relief, stone, and copper
25" x 15" x 2" (64 cm x 38 cm x 5 cm)

Apocalypse
hand-cut marble mosaic, stone, copper, and steel
24" x 26" (61 cm x 66 cm)

Annunziation I
hand-cut marble mosaic, stone, copper, and cement
36" x 30" x 2" (91 cm x 76 cm x 5 cm)

When You Travel East
hand-cut marble mosaic, stone, steel, and copper
25" x 3.4' (64 cm x 1 m)

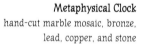

Metaphysical Clock
hand-cut marble mosaic, bronze,
lead, copper, and stone
28" x 24" x 2" (71 cm x 61 cm x 5 cm)

Ceramic Mosaic Panel

Commissioned by the New York City
Metropolitan Transportation Authority/Arts for Transit
96th Street Station, Lexington Avenue Subway, New York, New York
hand-cut marble mosaic
6' x 20" (1.8 m x 51 cm)

City Suite

Commissioned by the New York City
Metropolitan Transportation Authority/Arts for Transit
96th Street Station, Lexington Avenue Subway, New York, New York
hand-cut marble mosaic
4' x 4.5' (1.2 m x 1.4 m)

The Eastern Gate

hand-cut marble mosaic, stone, bronze, and ceramic
4' x 22" x 3" (1.2 m x 56 cm x 8 cm)

VERDIANO MARZI

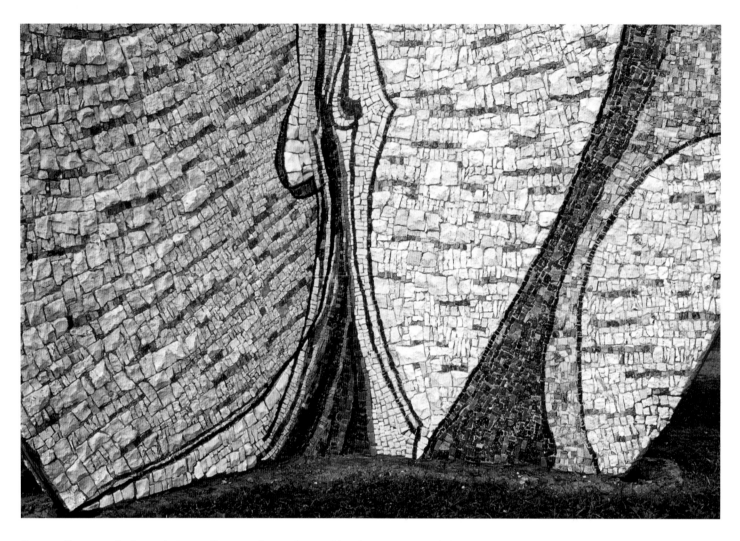

Born in Ravenna, Italy, and classically trained at such venerable institutions as the Ecole des Beaux-Arts and the Istituto d'Arte per il Mosaico, Verdiano Marzi's mosaics may be a surprise in their abstract style, but his approach to the art form remains true to tradition. "Since I was an eleven-year-old boy, I have been educated by the mosaicists of the Scuola di Ravenna. I was born there, in the city that was once the capital of the Byzantine Empire in the early Christian period," he attests.

Now a citizen of the Republic of San Marino, Marzi is dedicated to passing his skills on to the next generation.

In 1994, he developed and directed a workshop at the Louvre in Paris, France, introducing young people to mosaics. More recently, he traveled to Dahramsala, India, to teach Tibetan children the basics of the art.

Detail from **Nascita, face 1**

Creations by Verdiano Marzi can be divided into two categories: monumental works and private commissions. In the case of the former, the artist executes

TECHNIQUE

these installations personally but typically credits different painters with the designs of the mosaics. However, his private commissions are completely original. The jagged silhouettes often found in his freestanding pieces, as in the *Nascita*, and the rough-hewn stone central to many of his smaller works—*Le Repos*

des Météorites is one example—are his signature. They function as an arresting contrast in form and texture to the more regular *tesserae* that make up the remainder of the compositions.

With his pieces in collections in Germany, Japan, and throughout France, the artist maintains a well-rounded

Detail from **Virginia**

approach to his craft. Marzi has steeped himself in the very foundations of mosaics by participating in the restoration of paleo-Christian pavements in southern Italy, and nineteenth and twentieth-century floors in Paris.

Detail from **Le Repos des Meteorites**, marble, granite, and Venetian smalti

Nascita, face 2
park at Bourgouin Jallieu High School, France
marble, granite, and Venetian smalti
8.8' (2.7 m)

Sculptures
stone, marble, and concrete with
mosaic made of marble, granite,
and Venetian smalti
7.5' x 9.3' (2.3 m x 2.8 m)

Linea Dorata
marble, granite, and Venetian smalti
1.3' x 1.8' (.4 m x .5 m)

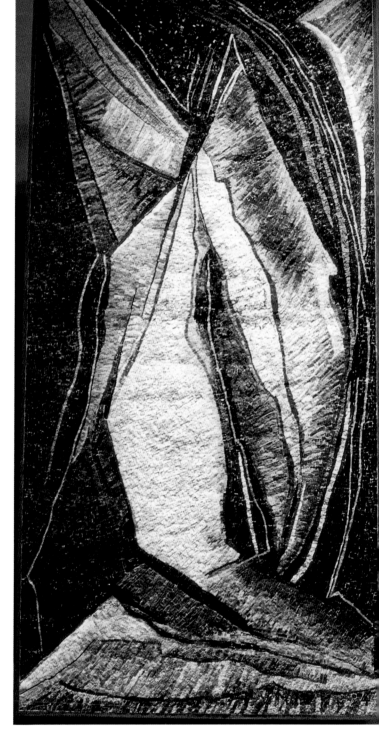

Interior Wall Mosaic
Mons Sarts Metro Station, Lille, France
marble, granite, and Venetian smalti
11.8' x 5.3' (3.6 m x 1.7 m)

St. George with Blue and Red Angels, triptych
(details below)
marble, granite, and Venetian smalti
9.3' x 3.5' (2.8 m x 1.1 m)

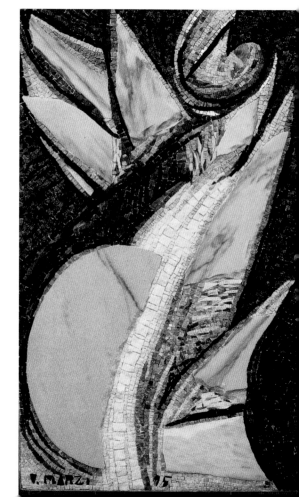

Still Life
marble, granite, and Venetian smalti
24" x 20" (60 cm x 50 cm)

Exterior Wall Mosaic
Mons Sarts Metro Station, Lille, France
marble, granite, and Venetian smalti
24" x 3.3' (60 cm x 1 m)

Mixed media works differ from traditional *tesserae*-based compositions in their 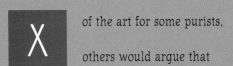 emphasis on the parts of the mosaic rather than the whole. While incorporating an amalgam of found objects may be straining the boundaries of the art for some purists, others would argue that the mixed-media artists profiled here satisfy a set of requisites far more fundamental: the urge to collect, compose, and create.

The bridge between ceramic mosaics and mixed-media mosaics is firmly anchored by a technique called *pique assiette* ("stolen from plates"). This name was first given to the ambitious folk art endeavor of Raymond Isidore, a Frenchman who spent nearly twenty-five years blanketing his entire home with shards of cast-off crockery and dishware. Completed in the 1960s, it heralded the new, freethinking age in the development of mosaic art.

Executors of this new age, the artists whose works follow all speak from different perspectives, yet they have a common voice. Ilana Shafir's mosaic window combinations, Jane Muir's landscape compositions, the Rosenbergs' carved concrete mosaic murals, Lynn Mattson's folk art, Twyla Arthur's architectural assemblages, Val Carroll's regional murals, Carlos Alves's ocean- and culture-derived pathways and murals, Candace Bahouth's mosaic transformation of mundane objects, and Isaiah Zagar's neighborhood monuments all use fragments that come together in one fashion or another, paying homage to nature.

LILLI ANN KILLEN ROSENBERG
Detail from
Children's Center Mural

ILANA SHAFIR
Detail from
Blessings

JANE MUIR
Detail from
Fruiting

CARLOS ALVES

Miami artist Carlos Alves creates wildly imaginative floors, ceilings, and walls. While Miami is host to most of his works, his signature creations are permanent installations in such far-off places as London, Hong Kong, and, closer to home, New York City.

With more than a decade of successful projects ranging from interior works to ceramic portraits to transit stations and swimming pools to his credit, the question of commercial production arises. Alves offers a sure response: "I could be mass-producing furniture, but I disregard that idea because I don't want my pieces to lose their integrity. I want them to be special and have their dignity." Not surprisingly, the artist also has a decidedly upfront attitude about the goals of his mosaics. "I want people to have to interact with my work, to consider it, and to consider what it makes them think about. If I succeed, then I feel like I've really accomplished something."

Private Bathroom
handmade ceramic, stained glass, and mirror

Carlos Alves spends a lot of time breaking and reconfiguring old ceramics, which he then uses as individual pieces in larger designs. Greatly attracted by

TECHNIQUE

the concept of recycling, Alves takes pleasure in reusing old bits and likes the idea of breaking down the pristine and fragile wholeness of an individual ceramic piece.

Detail from **Atlantis**, *South Florida Art Center*, assorted tile

Alves's works are closely connected to his childhood in the Miami Beach area. His Cuban roots, abundant, flowing gardens, and the years he spent in the ocean collecting shells and diving all merge together as inspiration for the spiral sea creatures and Latin symbolism that appear in his mosaics. His latest venture is exploring portraiture. Working with recycled china pieces, Alves is starting to create huge images of individuals.

Detail from **Señorita Margarita**

Sirena
handmade ceramic tile
26' x 6' x 14" (7.9 m x 1.8 m x 36 cm)

Save the Waters
marble, tile, and metal
1,200 square feet (360 square meters)

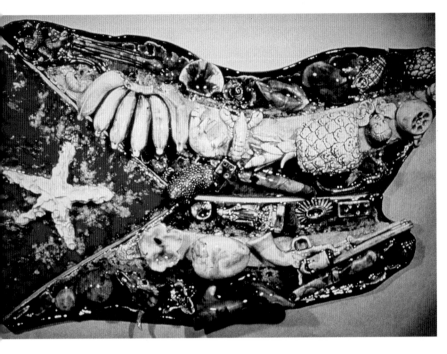

Cuban Flag
recycled ceramic tile
3.3' x 32" x 6" (1 meter x 81 cm x 15 cm)

Map of South Florida (detail)
Everglades National Park
marble, hand-glazed ceramic tile, and brass
630 square feet (189 square meters)

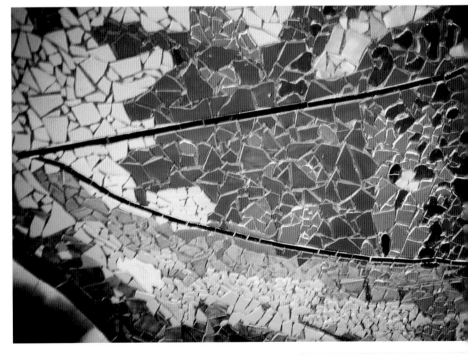

Señorita Margarita
recycled ceramic tile and fused glass
24" x 24" (60 cm x 60 cm)

Most of Twyla Arthur's mosaics are site-specific, permanent installations, as much a part of the architecture of a building or landscape as an embellishment. This type of relationship stems from the fluidity of her work and her ability to create art that is often functional and always respectful of the space it occupies.

Trained in fine arts at Mills College, Arthur initially concentrated on sculpture and painting, but for the last ten years, assemblage has been her medium. Her mosaics include man-made ceramics and glass—however, more often than not, rock and natural stone predominate. In gardens, patios, and outdoor environments, this choice emphasizes the rustic ambience of the settings; in more refined contexts, it introduces an element of contrast. In either situation, texture takes the lead—hefty chunks, water-smoothed slabs, and pebbly surfaces invite people to touch as well as view.

Detail from **Mosaic Sidewalk**

Twyla Arthur is influenced and moved to create by primitive architecture and vernacular art. "I love the mud houses of West Africa because as an art form they

TECHNIQUE

are part of the culture, not contrived like much of western art. Traditionally women's art, the houses are sculptural in shape and painted with rich designs and colors. Their tools are primitive—most of the work is done with their hands," Arthur says.

Her work for both the terrace and interior of architect David Baker's house in Berkeley, California, reinforces her philosophy. Stones on the multilevel terrace are laid out in a flowing, organic pattern supportive of the material. Inlaid nuts, bolts, and other construction materials are a lighthearted reference to the building process, conjuring up images of an unearthed foundation. Inside the house, broken marble, concrete, and ceramic

Detail from **Bathroom**

shards are laid by hand to create their own primitive sensibility in the kitchen and the bath.

Detail from **Mosaic Spoons**

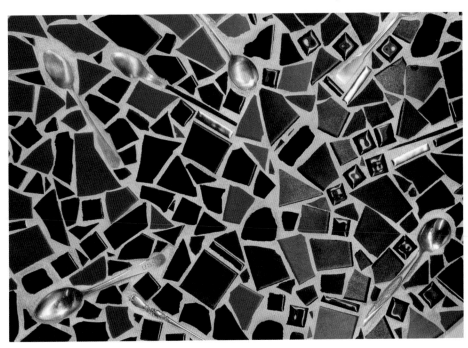

Concrete Mosaic Rug
Lobby Interior
concrete tile handmade by Buddy Rhodes
36" x 12' (90 cm x 3.7 m)

Mosaic Fork
UC Berkeley, Unit I Dining Hall
ceramic tile
6' x 18" (1.8 m x 46 cm)

Ceramic Tile Bench
UC Berkeley, residence hall
8' x 28" (2.4 m x 71 cm)

Bathroom
David Baker residence
ceramic tile and mirrors

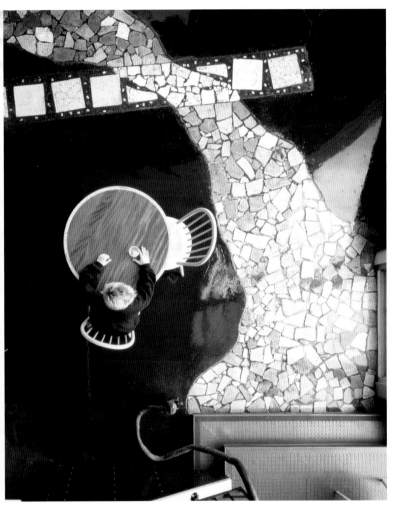

Mosaic Floor
Bison Brewing Company
concrete tile handmade by Buddy Rhodes
100 square feet (30 square meters)

Detail from **Mosaic Floor**

CANDACE BAHOUTH

An accomplished textile artist, Candace Bahouth originally earned her reputation by weaving tapestry portraits with a three-dimensional presence to them. This attracted the curators at the Victoria and Albert Museum in London, who acquired several of these innovative pieces for their collection. The next phase of her work was devoted to intricate needlepoint designs based on medieval motifs and symbols. Eventually, these designs were turned into a successful line of commercial craft kits. Then, for a brief moment, the artist turned her attention to mosaics, but she became so enamored that she has kept her eyes (and her hands) firmly fixed on this art form ever since.

Contrary to what one might expect, the transition between needle artistry and mosaics is not a great leap for Bahouth. Both media are pattern-oriented, both are essentially additive processes involving very small components, and in this artist's case, both rely on a dynamic use of color for maximum effect.

Details from **Cabinet** (above and opposite)

Fiber and mosaic artist Candace Bahouth could be speaking of silk threads or ceramic *tesserae* when she says, "I have a fascination with fragments and the

TECHNIQUE

redemptive metamorphosis of a thing quite ordinary into something wonderful, extraordinary, even nonsensical, amusing— an object of delight."

Transformation of the mundane into a fanciful mosaic monument is her hallmark. One brilliant example is a simple pedestal birdbath that she covered with a thick impasto of color-coordinated

Detail from **Porcelain Head**

grout embedded with brilliant shards of mirror, glass, and ceramic. This common garden element has re-emerged as an extravagant ornament. A slight spin on

this eclectic aesthetic is the treatment she gives to a stone fence in the English countryside. The pattern of rough grey rubble is broken without warning by a vertical vein of fractured cobalt tile, an impetuous contrast to the otherwise tranquil setting that underscores

Detail from **Large Urn**

Bahouth's outlook regarding the environment. "Nature is one of life's most intense, emotional experiences, the most perfect of worlds, my main inspiration and dwelling place."

Stone Wall
broken china
14" x 30" (36 cm x 76 cm)

Cabinet
broken china and tile
28" x 4.4' x 15"
(71 cm x 1.3 m x 38 cm)

Confetti Vase
broken china and tile
12" x 8" diameter
(30 cm x 20 cm diameter)

Small Picture Frame
shells, turquoise stones, and gold leaf
10" square (25 cm square)

Large Urn
broken china, *tesserae*, and mirror
4.4' x 27" diameter (1.3 m x 69 cm diameter)

Porcelain Head
tesserae bits
22" x 18" x 10" (56 cm x 46 cm x 25 cm)

Porch with Medieval Mullion Window
cement and shells
5.6' x 9.6' (1.7 m x 2.9 m)

Egyptian Table
iron, cement, tesserae, and gold leaf
25" x 13" x 19"
(64 cm x 33 cm x 48 cm)

Pillar and Ball
broken china, mirror, and tile
5.8' x 14" square (1.8 m x 36 cm square)

VAL CARROLL

For nearly ten years, Val Carroll and her mosaics have been a growing presence in the Caribbean, where a number of vacation resorts have commissioned her to design, fabricate, and install large-scale projects that evoke images of nature, often as part of swimming pool or spa facilities. Just as dramatic, but less frequently on public display, are the artist's unique mosaic sculptures. Although stationary and inanimate, these abstract renditions of flora and fauna always appear to be in motion. Both *Afternoon Delight* and *Unlikely Menage x 3* depict the tidewater life that Carroll favors for her site installations.

Carroll has worked almost strictly in mosaics for the last eighteen years, but her earlier experience in painting, weaving, and sculpture is constantly being reconfigured, resulting in new directions for the evolution of her mosaics.

Detail from **Tidal Treasures, Fire Coral**

"Since childhood, I have had a fascination with biology and the natural world," says Carroll. That innate attraction, coupled with the 1970s attitudes about regionalism

TECHNIQUE

and the importance of preserving the unique aspects of local cultures, have greatly influenced Carroll's work through the years. "Nature remains my favorite source of inspiration," she states, and often she finds herself outside, dealing with both the joys and the discomfort nature has to offer.

One of her most important works, *Tidal Treasures*, an 18,000-square-foot

Detail from **Tidal Treasures**, Anemone

(5,400-square-meter) underwater mural, was months in the making. Humidity and island heat, along with dust and construction debris from the concurrent renovation of the adjacent hotel, made this her most challenging project, which

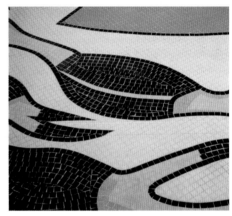

Detail from **Tidal Treasures**, Seaweed

the artist likens to "installing tile on a barbecue." But the tropical setting of Santa Lucia provided the artist with ideal inspiration—her mural depicts the region's colossal tide pool creatures like starfish and anemones, as well as fire coral, seaweed, and reef plants.

Detail from **Tidal Treasures**, Sand Dollar

Tidal Treasures
porcelain mosaic
18,000 square feet (5,400 square meters)

Detail from **Tidal Treasures**

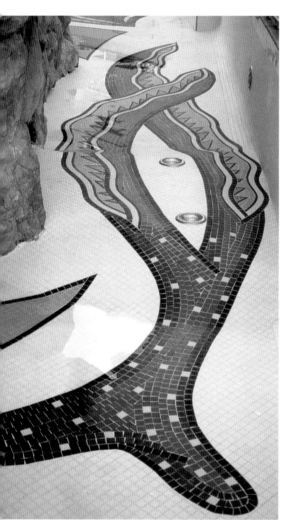

Tidal Treasures, Sea Sponge
porcelain mosaic
28' x 7' (8.5 m x 2.1 m)

Tidal Treasures, Shell (under bridge)
porcelain mosaic
25' x 12' (7.6 m x 3.7 m)

GALLERY

Serendipidus
glass mosaic and mixed media
5' x 30' x 5" (1.5 m x 9.1 m x 13 cm)

Serendipidus I (below)
glass mosaic and mixed media
5" x 33" x 6.75' (13 cm x 84 cm x 2.1 m)

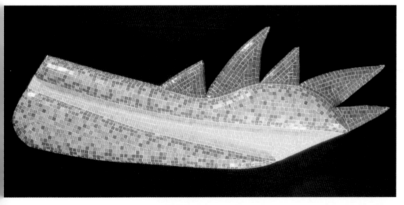

Serendipidus II
glass mosaic and mixed media
5" x 21" x 32" (13 cm x 53 cm x 81 cm)

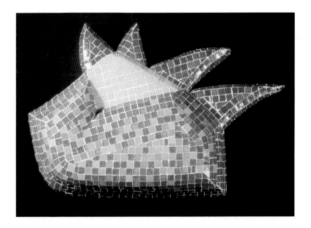

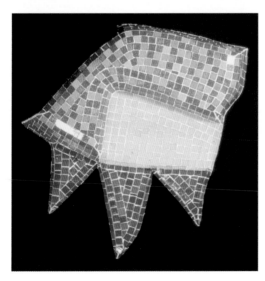

Serendipidus IV
glass mosaic and mixed media
5" x 27" x 23"
(13 cm x 68 cm x 58 cm)

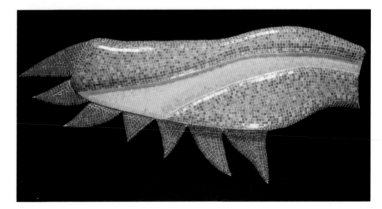

Serendipidus III
glass mosaic and mixed media
5" x 4.75' x 9' (13 cm x 1.5 m x 2.7 m)

Afternoon Delight
ceramic mosaic, steel, and concrete
12' x 10' (3.7 m x 3 m)

Details from **Afternoon Delight**
(above left and left)

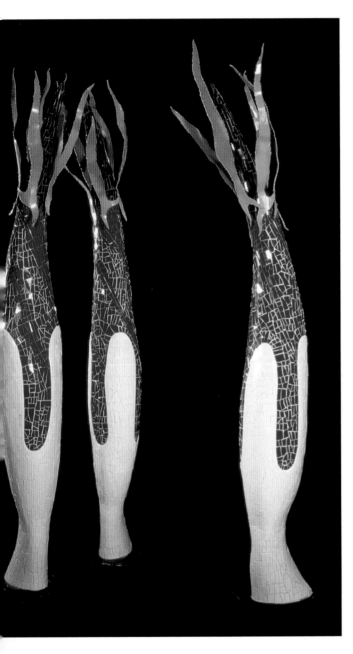

Unlikely Menage x 3
ceramic mosaic, steel, and concrete
11' x 4' x 2.5' (3.4 m x 1.2 m x .8 m)

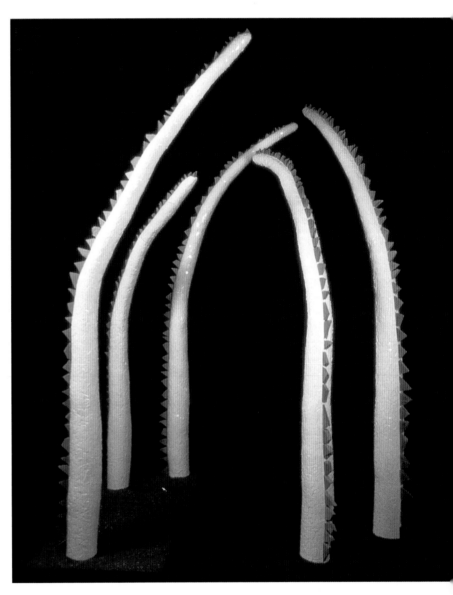

Awakenings, 5 pieces, exterior installation
ceramic mosaic, terra cotta, concrete, and steel
9' x 8" (2.7 m x 20 cm) each

LYNN MATTSON

Lynn Mattson assembles chipped and cracked fragments of antique china, pottery, and figurines into constructions that tell a story. The secrets and compelling history of each time-worn bit are given new meaning with the artist's take on "memoryware," a popular form of American folk art from the early 1900s in which women affixed their keepsakes to containers. With her functional teapots, cookie jars, vases, and other sculptural pieces, Mattson continues this fanciful tradition of artistic narrative.

Born in San Francisco in 1958, Mattson has an extensive background in textiles and sculpted wall pieces. Her training as an artist began in seventh grade when she was sent to live in a convent for three years. One of the nuns had a giant ceramics studio, and Mattson spent most of her time there. A gift of a kiln a short time later cast her future in clay.

Detail from **Pisa**

The most important influence on Lynn Mattson's artwork is the subject she happens to be teaching at the time in her hands-on children's art history class.

TECHNIQUE

"It could be Baroque, Asian, Old World Italian, or the art of the circus," explains Mattson, "but whatever the topic, that is where I focus all of my creative energies in order to capture the true essence of the art theme."

With these shifting influences, she changes her materials. Grainy, dull green mortar binds together pieces with

Detail from **Childhood Memories, cookie jar**

Detail from **Alexandria**

personal significance—the subdued tones, says Mattson, are contemplative and allow the importance of the individual

tesserae to be fully appreciated. When evoking an entire culture or era, the overall impact of the piece is heightened with bright hues such as electric blue or magenta. Like the memoryware of old, the worn and broken pieces that Mattson uses in her work tell her story. But in a

Detail from **Hallelujah**

departure from the manner of thinking of the Victorian housewives who started this craft, Mattson's vibrant constructions offer a perspective that looks toward the future.

Pisa
ceramic and mixed media
19" x 9" (48 cm x 23 cm)

Childhood Memories, cookie jar
ceramic and mixed media
12" x 8" (30 cm x 20 cm)

Misha
ceramic and mixed media
6" x 9" (15 cm x 23 cm)

Alexandria
ceramic and mixed media
15" x 12" (38 cm x 30 cm)

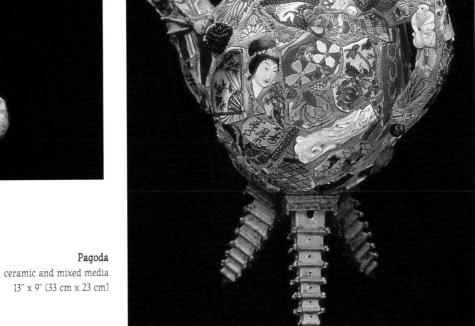

Luster Tree
ceramic and mixed media
20" x 10" (51 cm x 25 cm)

Pagoda
ceramic and mixed media
13" x 9" (33 cm x 23 cm)

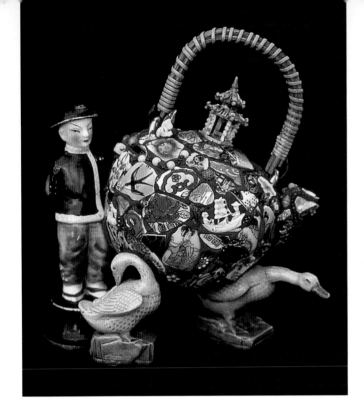

Ping
ceramic and mixed media
6" x 9" (15 cm x 23 cm)

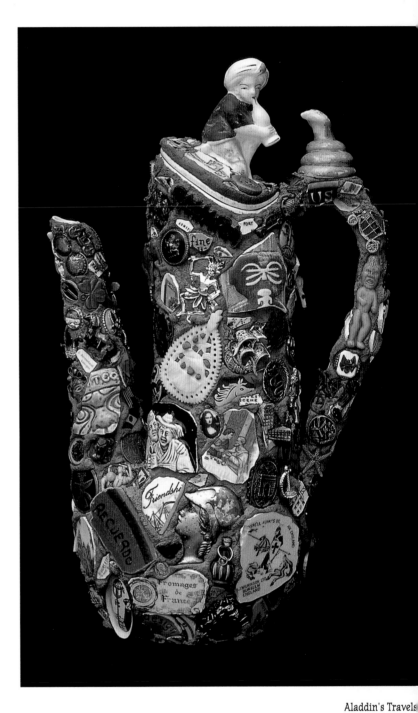

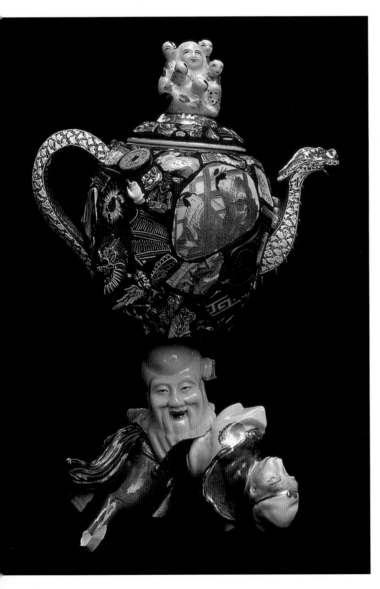

Aladdin's Travels
ceramic and mixed media
16" x 12" (41 cm x 30 cm)

Floating Island
ceramic and mixed media
14" x 9" (36 cm x 23 cm)

Travel Log USA
ceramic and mixed media
12" x 9" (30 cm x 23 cm)

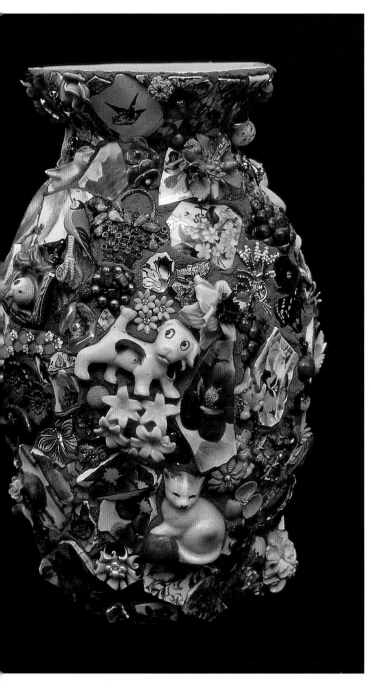

Grandma's Garden, San Anselmo, California
ceramic and mixed media
16" x 8" (41 cm x 20 cm)

Mexican Bean Pot
ceramic and mixed media
11" x 12" (28 cm x 30 cm)

While studying medieval history at Oxford University, Jane Muir took a trip to Italy and encountered the mosaics at Ravenna, which she much admired. Her work as a mosaic artist, however, did not begin until she could no longer stand the sight of an ugly coal house door that was in clear view whenever she stood at her sink to wash dishes or clean up after two small children. With no experience, but a lot of panache, that door was boldly transformed with an Indian Tree of Life motif.

She was in her late thirties before she formally studied art—painting, sculpture, murals, and mosaics. Despite her fascination with mosaics, Muir discovered few people who shared her enthusiasm, and most even purposefully avoided it. When she set up a studio in 1968, she realized that mosaics were typically associated with "nasty coffee-tabletop kits of vitreous materials in garish colors." At that point, Muir decided to devote her career to changing such opinions and educating the public about mosaic design as an art form.

Detail from **Fruiting**

Jane Muir creates dramatically textured mosaic landscape compositions. Nature, its symbolism, and folklore exert a strong influence on her work, and many of the

TECHNIQUE

patterns she assembles suggest topographical maps or geological formations. Muir works with diverse materials, unexpectedly juxtaposing contrasts of texture, color, and reflective elements.

Rough-hewn slate, brick, gold leaf, lead crystal, and brilliant Venetian smalti find their way into the pieces she executes in high relief. Light is the most critical element to the success of her art.

Detail from **The Leaves Be Green**

Clusters and rivers of chunky *tesserae* are deliberately sculptured into her mosaics for depth and shadow, to maneuver light where she wants it.

The influences of Botticelli, Rembrandt, Tapies, Paul Klee, and Romanesque carvings are all formative references that she says have seen her through the development of her work.

Detail from **Happy Birds**

But this artist is most influenced by the often abstract qualities of the natural environment. Weathered rocks, the sea, and mythical animals remain compelling sources of inspiration that she constantly reaches out to, for, she says, "The excitement lies in the search."

Detail from **Canterbury Longmarket**

JANE MUIR

Fruiting
glass mosaic, slate, and tile
19.5" x 20" (50 cm x 51 cm)

Canterbury Longmarket
mosaic pavement, marble, high-fired stoneware,
and Venetian smalti
59 square feet (18 square meters)

The Leaves Be Green
Venetian smalti, glass fusion, green
slate, and gold leaf
20" x 15" (51 cm x 38 cm)

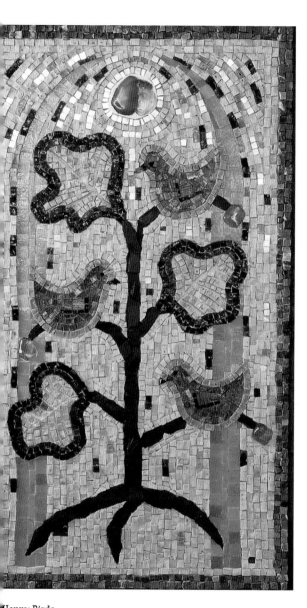

Happy Birds
slate, glass fusion, and Venetian smalti
36" x 21" (92 cm x 54 cm)

Great Cascade
slate and Venetian smalti
25" x 16" (64 cm x 40 cm)

Muralist, sculptor, and potter, Lilli Ann Killen Rosenberg is best known for her public art projects that help to enliven the cities of Boston and New York. What sets Rosenberg's work apart is the high level of community participation that she seeks for her concrete mosaic commissions. Such collaboration culminates in highly acclaimed "art in public places" that integrates the needs of a community with its architectural environment.

Frequently working with husband Marvin Rosenberg, a social worker, Lilli Ann Killen Rosenberg creates pieces layered with both personal meaning and universal significance. Much of Rosenberg's work is devoted or related to children and children's themes. Her largest commission to date is the MBTA's Park Street Station in Boston, *Celebration of the Underground*. Commemorating the opening of the first American subway in 1897, the mural is a sprawling, graphic narrative, the result of extensive interviews the artist conducted with historians, geologists, motormen, and mechanics.

Details from **Celebration of the Underground**
(above and opposite page)

Lilli Ann Killen Rosenberg's mosaic murals are created in concrete. More than just a supporting structure, it is itself an art medium, often colored and textured.

TECHNIQUE

Sometimes carved into sculpture or cast, concrete serves as Rosenberg's invitation for community involvement. "It is the perfect medium for people of all ages to make clay pieces, collect objects, and contribute their skills for a collaborative collage, resulting in a shared sense of ownership," says Rosenberg.

She first started using concrete when working on a children's art program in New York City. She was so

inspired by their clay pieces that she embedded them into murals, sculpture gardens, and paved areas. The joyful spirit and delight in the children's imaginations helped Rosenberg brighten some very dim neighborhoods.

Like the artist's finished compositions, concrete is indestructible, and both simple and complex. Viewers are invited

to touch the works for a tactile experience that will linger in their memories, much like the lasting impression the mosaics from the Watts Tower, a Southern California folk art dream palace, made on Rosenberg when she was a teenager.

Celebration of the Underground
MBTA Park Street Station, Boston, Massachusetts
ceramic, glass, metal, and mixed media
10' x 110' (3 m x 33.5 m)

Details from **Celebration of the Underground**
(above and right)

Children's Center Mural
Four Seasons, Philadelphia, Pennsylvania
concrete mosaic, found objects,
mixed media, and ceramic
18' x 36' (5.5 m x 11 m)

Details from **Children's Center Mural**

ILANA SHAFIR

For Ilana Shafir, the first step on the path to her life as an artist was taken among simple peasants in a tiny Yugoslavian village where her family sought refuge from the Nazis. A seventeen-year-old, she was so affected by the courage and strength of these villagers that she began to paint their portraits and the landscape. Born in Sarajevo, Shafir attended the Zagreb Academy of Arts after the war. In 1949, she immigrated to Israel and settled in Ashkelon to work as an artist and teacher, and there she began creating mosaics.

The Netzach Israel Synagogue in Ashkelon is brightened by Shafir's unique signature—a stained glass window and mosaic combination within a single frame. This dual-form mosaic is designed around the daily ebb and flow of light—bright Mediterranean daylight passes through the glass and then slowly fades into the night's shadows, giving center stage to the opaque *tesserae*. This aesthetic interplay and transformation of light make Shafir's mosaics easily identifiable.

Detail from **Jerusalem** (above and opposite)

Primarily a self-taught mosaicist, Ilana Shafir's works are fabricated from a variety of traditional and unexpected materials. These include seashells,

TECHNIQUE

ceramic pieces, broken china, natural stones, pebbles, minerals, and gold and silver tesserae. Her mosaics have a spiritual atmosphere characterized by a dynamic flow upward toward the sky. Her materials inspire her artworks: "There is always a one-of-a-kind stone, piece of ceramic, or broken handle with

Detail from **Jerusalem**
(includes the sign "Z" that the artist and her sister wore as Jewesses during World War II)

Detail from **The Big Gate**

which I begin my work. The mosaic grows with its own laws of composition and texture but is always related to that first piece."

After thirty years as an artist in her community, Shafir has ready sources of materials. "All the town knows that my studio is the address to deposit broken ceramics. From time to time, someone stands admiring one of my mosaics and says, 'Now I see what she has done with my broken china set!'"

Jerusalem
colored glass from Murano, broken ceramic, and found objects
5.8' x 36" (1.8 m x 90 cm)

The Closed Gate
gold smalti, marble *tesserae*, shells,
corals, broken ceramic, pebbles,
found objects, and sandstone
32" x 24" (80 cm x 60 cm)

Star
ceramic, pebbles, shells, green
eilat stones, and gold and silver smalti
20" x 28" (50 cm x 70 cm)

The Big Gate
gold smalti, marble *tesserae*, basalt, granite, eilat, arad, and alabaster stones,
broken ceramic, pebbles, shells, and corals
32" x 4' (80 cm x 1.2 m)

Wedding
broken and cut ceramic and corals
16" x 20" (40 cm x 50 cm)

The Soil of Ashkelon
stone *tesserae*, natural stones, pebbles, broken
ceramic, ceramic tiles, and handmade ceramic par
9.8' x 8.3' (3 m x 2.5 m)

**Mural at the Entrance Wall of the
Woldenberg Community Center, Ashkelon**
stone *tesserae*, natural stones,
pebbles, broken ceramic, ceramic tiles,
and handmade ceramic parts
10' x 6.5' (3 m x 2 m)

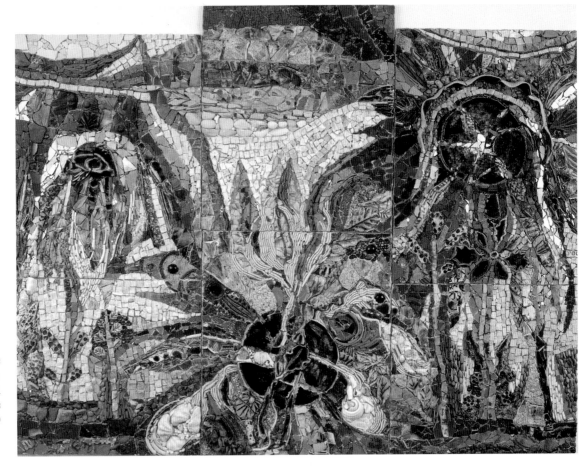

Blessings
broken ceramic, handmade ceramic parts,
pebbles, marble *tesserae*, gold and
silver smalti, glass, corals, and shells
5.8' x 4.8' (1.8 m x 1.4 m)

Garden
handmade ceramic parts, broken ceramic, and marble *tesserae*
36" x 24" (90 cm x 60 cm)

The Flower Gate
broken ceramic, stone *tesserae*, gold smalti, pebbles, and glass
27" x 31" (68 cm x 78 cm)

ISAIAH ZAGAR

For more than twenty-five years, Isaiah Zagar has been fashioning an extensive body of folk art, embellishing interior and exterior walls throughout Philadelphia with mosaics. Although at first the public looked askance at his murals, these works are now highly acclaimed and much admired for their rich contribution to the city's fabric. Zagar has transformed at least twenty bland and dispirited settings in the South Street and Old City neighborhoods into enclaves of surprise and delight. While not physically connected, these wall murals establish a distinct public art environment that Zagar calls a psychically contiguous system of parks.

Originally trained as a printmaker and painter, Zagar studied at the Pratt Institute in Brooklyn, New York, and then switched to mosaics. His executions are not purely architectural ornaments, for they embody an individual aesthetic and a strong, unified vision, one that turns nondescript architecture into colorful sculpture.

Detail from **Kater Street Studio**

Isaiah Zagar's mosaic installations transform masonry facades, walls, and stairwells that were once expressionless into dazzling abstractions of tile, mirror, and

TECHNIQUE

found objects. Every surface is completely covered, painted in minute and imaginative detail. Embedded into his murals are spiraling, twisted, or upside down messages from Zagar spelled out in pieces of broken mirror or tile. Despite the large size of his projects—up to 6,000 square feet (540 square meters)—Zagar works without a plan.

Greatly influenced by the rich, distinctive colors found in the cultures of

Detail from **A Day in America**

South America, where he worked for five years as a craft developer with the Peace Corps, Zagar adopted these brilliant hues into his own work. He uses these colorful references as a cultural link, believing that art is a universal language capable of joining widely disparate peoples. The influence of Marcel Duchamp, Antonio Gaudi, and outsider artists can also be seen in his mosaics. Zagar's work has been referred to as an artistic expression of the concept that things don't need to be "either/or"—instead they can be both/and."

Detail from **Kater Street Studio**

Kater Street Studio,
entranceway interior
tile mosaic
12' x 15' (3.7 m x 4.6 m)

Kater Street Studio, Canopy on South
Street side
mixed media mosaic
30' x 40' (9.1 m x 12.2 m)

Kater Street Studio, exterior
mixed media mosaic
20' x 30' (6.1 m x 9.1 m)

Pemberton Street Wall
mixed media mosaic
12' x 25' (3.7 m x 7.6 m)

Mildred Street Wall
mixed media mosaic
8' x 30' (2.4 m x 9.1 m)

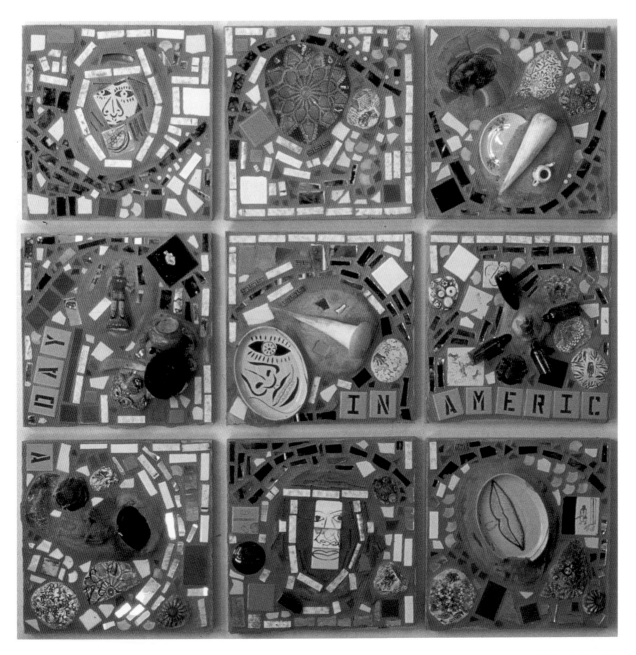

A Day in America
mixed media
88" x 88" (224 cm x 224 cm)

GALLERY OF ARTISTS

Waving Strings
natural stones and
colored cement
4' x 32" (1.2 m x 80 cm)

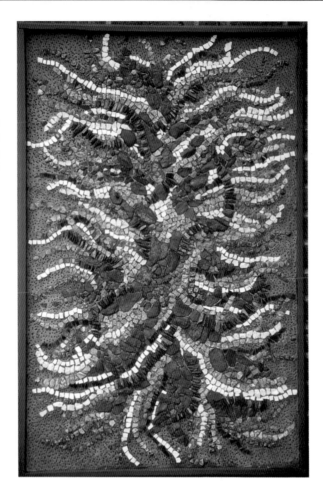

HARRIET BACKER

Detail from **Fire**, glass and gold

MARLO BARTELS

Catalan Fish Fountain
ceramic tile and ferro cement
8' x 7' x 3.5' (2.4 m x 2.1 m x 1.1 m)

Ceramic Tile Mural
Home Savings of America, Pembroke Pines, Florida
8' x 12' (2.4 m x 3.7 m)

PATTY DETZER

After Van der Weyden
clay and found objects
24" x 24" (60 cm x 60 cm)

Greenhouse and Aviary
mosaic collage and handmade tiles
6' x 26" (1.8 m x 66 cm)

BARBARA FIELD

Dream's Peak (right)
mosaic tile panels
6.7' x 24" (2 m x 60 cm) each

Shaharazad
mosaic tile
40' x 3.5' (12.2 m x 1.1 m)

MERLE FISHMAN AND DAVID CATRAMBONE
Venus
glass and marble
3' x 11' (.9 m x 3.4 m)

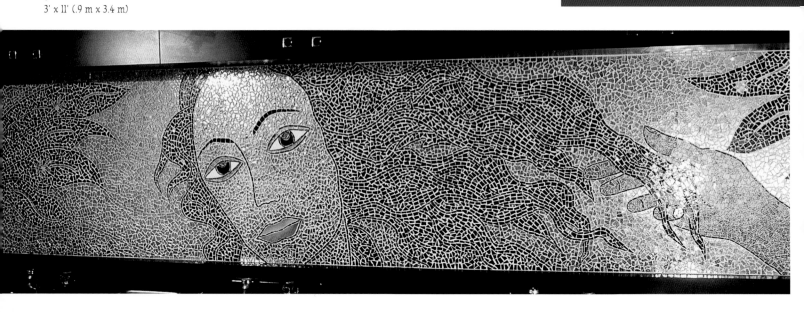

MERLE FISHMAN AND
DAVID CATRAMBONE
The Wave
ceramic tile
5' x 9' (1.5 m x 2.7 m)

DAVID CATRAMBONE
Crucifix
linoleum mosaic
8' x 4' (2.4 m x 1.2 m)

ANN GARDNER

Danza del Cerchio (below, detail below left)
Port of Seattle, Washington
glass mosaic, 11' x 43' (3.4 m x 13.1 m)

PETER KASKIEWICZ

Valley Vikings
Valley High School, Albuquerque, New Mexico
ceramic and glass tiles, found objects,
gemstones, and seashells
10' x 10' (3 m x 3 m)

Union Square
14th Street Subway, New York, New York
marble, granite, onyx, slate, sandstone, brick,
old tiles, Italian glass, and tumbled glass beads
5.5' x 8.6' (1.7 m x 2.6 m)

Detail from **Screen of Four Seasons, Summer**
marble, gold, silver, and smalti

Earth of Delight and Sorrow
marble, gold, silver, and cocciopesto
3' x 24" x 24" (.9 m x 60 cm x 60 cm)

GLEN MICHAELS

Detail from **Assemblage**
AIA Headquarters, Detroit, Michigan
tile, cameo glass, and bronze

Detail from **Assemblage** (left)
Detroit Receiving Hospital, Michigan
tile and metal

GIFFORD MYERS

Remark *(Le Monde Rien)*
glaze on clay
5' x 6' x 20" diameter
(1.5 m x 1.8 m x 51 cm diameter)

Poolside with Red Ball (left)
glaze on clay and flagstone
5' x 5.5' x 20" diameter
(1.5 m x 1.7 m x 51 cm diameter)

Details from **The Rosalie Doolittle Fountain**
(above and right)
Rio Grande Botanic Garden, Albuquerque, New Mexico
ceramic and tile mosaic

Angels Tend My Garden, table
ceramic
4' x 3' x 3' (1.2 m x .9 m x .9 m)

PEDRO ROMERO

New Mexico Low Rider Bench
ceramic on cement
5' x 16' x 4' (1.5 m x 4.9 m x 1.2 m)

APRIL SHELDON

Patio and Outside Fireplace
(right and below)
Carmel, California
ceramic tile mosaic

He Speaks of Possible Futures
rhinestone, mosaic, and mixed media
19" x 10" x 4" (48 cm x 25 cm x 10 cm)

JOAN DI STEFANO RUIZ

Fireplace (above, detail left)
natural stone, ceramic tile, glass, mica, and crystals
6' x 3.9' x 6" (1.8 m x 1.2 m x 15 cm)

Home Sweet Home
ceramic mosaic and found objects
5.6' x 14" x 11" (1.7 m x 36 cm x 28 cm)

Detail from **Clock of Ages**
ceramic mosaic and found objects

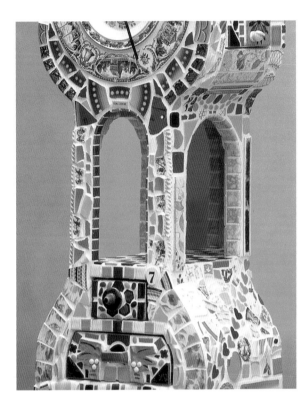

Exploded: dining table
ceramic and granite
29" x 9.2' x 3.5' (74 cm x 2.8 m x 1.1 m)

Slipped Covers
chairs with granite inlay and copper edging
3.3' x 20" x 20" (1 m x 51 cm x 51 cm)

Erin Adams
5551 Florence Terrace
Oakland, CA 94611
United States

Carlos Alves
1043 Lincoln Road
Miami Beach, FL 33139
United States

Twyla Arthur
2007 W. Summit
San Antonio, TX 78209
United States

Harriet Backer
Heyerdahlsrei 18
0386 Oslo, Norway

Candace Bahouth
Ebenezer Chapel
Pilton, Somerset
BA4 4BR
England

Marlo Bartels
2307 Laguna Canyon Road, #7
Laguna Beach, CA 92651
United States

Linda Beaumont
1517 12th Avenue
Seattle, WA 98122
United States

Ellen Blakeley
3244 Folsom Street
San Francisco, CA 94110
United States

Joseph Blue Sky and Donna Webb
943 Dopler Street
Akron, OH 44303
United States

Laura Bradley
241 West Broadway
New York, NY 10013
United States

Val Carroll
6040 SW 28th Street
Miami, FL 33155
United States

Patty Detzer
2083 Fir Island Road
Mt. Vernon, WA 98273
United States

Barbara Field
473 Medicine Bow Road
Aspen, CO 81611
United States

Merle Fishman
David Catrambone
Projectile
4630 Saloma Avenue
Sherman Oaks, CA 91403
United States

Ann Gardner
4136 Meridian Avenue N
Seattle, WA 98103
United States

Peter Kaskiewicz
Apricot Salmon Productions
5110 1/2 Guadalupe Trail, NW
Albuquerque, NM 87107
United States

Gloria Kosco
P.O. Box 223
Silverdale, PA 18962
United States

Edith Kramer
95 Vandam Street, Apt. 3F
New York, NY 10013
United States

Haruya Kudo
7-7-9-202
Togashira, Toride
302 Japan

Verdiano Marzi
14, rue Louise-Michel
93170 Bagnolet
France

Lynn Mattson
25302 Calle Becerra
Laguna Niguel, CA 92677
United States

Glen Michaels
4800 Beach Road
Troy, MI 48098
United States

Jane Muir
Butcher's Orchard, Main Street
Weston Turville
Aylesbury, Bucks
HP22 5RL
England

Gifford Myers
1267 Boston Street
Altadena, CA 91001
United States

Shel Neymark
P.O. Box 25
Embudo, NM 87531
United States

Felice Nittolo
Via A. Codronchi, 61
48100 Ravenna
Italy

Lucio Orsoni
Cannaregio, 1045
30121 Venice
Italy

Cathy Raingarden
c/o Christensen Heller Gallery
5831 College Avenue
Oakland, CA 94618
United States

Pedro Romero
P.O. Box 16422
Santa Fe, NM 87506
United States

Lilli Ann Killen Rosenberg
Marvin Rosenberg
4001 Little Applegate Road
Jacksonville, OR 97530
United States

Diana Maria Rossi
1747 Oregon Street
Berkeley, CA 94703
United States

Ilana Shafir
Kapstadt Str. 2
Ashkelon 78406
Israel

April Sheldon
477 Bryant Street
San Francisco, CA 94107
United States

Beryl Solla
1222 N.W. 83rd Avenue
Coral Springs, FL 33071
United States

Mark Soppeland
576 Fairhill Drive
Akron, OH 44313
United States

Joan di Stefano Ruiz
P.O. Box 24605
Oakland, CA 94623
United States

Gary Stephens
36 Martens Boulevard
San Rafael, CA 94901
United States

Robert Stout
Stephanie Jurs
Twin Dolphin Mosaics
10 Barker Avenue
Fairfax, CA 94930
United States

Zoe and Steve Terlizzese
511 46th Street
West Palm Beach, FL 33407
United States

Nina Yankowitz
106 Spring Street
New York, NY 10012
United States

Isaiah Zagar
c/o Synderman Gallery
(Rick Synderman)
303 Cherry Street
Philadelphia, PA 19106
United States

PHOTOGRAPHY CREDITS

Erin Adams (p. 10)

Tapestry/Rug, Radisson Empire Hotel
Tapestry/Rug, Cynthia Steffe Showroom
Photos by Jennifer Levy

Carlos Alves (p. 86)

Private bathroom
Photo by Jonathan Rachline/
Photographers 2, Inc.

Twyla Arthur (p. 90)

Concrete mosaic rug
Photo by Roger Allen Lee

David Baker residence
Photos by Allen Weintraub
and Claudio Santini

Mosaic sidewalk at Alamo Children's
Advocacy Center, San Antonio, Texas
Photos by Leigh McLeod

Candace Bahouth (p. 94)

Stone Wall
Photo by Ian Sumner

Porch with medieval mullion window
Photo by Steven Morgan

Cabinet
Photo by David Cripps

Detail of cabinet and Egyptian table
Photos by James Merrell

Large urn and confetti vase
Photos by David Cripps

Porcelain head
Photos by Andreas von Einsiedel

Marlo Bartels (p. 132)

Ceramic tile mural,
Home Savings of America,
Pembroke Pines, Florida
Photo by Mark Sanderson

Catalan fish fountain
Photo by Mark Sanderson

Linda Beaumont (p. 66)

Water for Fire, Bailey Boushay, entry vestibule,
AIDS Hospice
Photo by Eduardo Calderon

Joseph Blue Sky and Donna Webb (p. 38)

King Triton and the Little Mermaid,
Children's Hospital, Akron, Ohio;

Magic Fountain, Metro Health Center,
Cleveland, Ohio
Photos by Heather Protz

Laura Bradley (p. 72)

City Suite and Ceramic Mosaic Panel,
New York City Metropolitan Transportation
Authority/Arts for Transit
96th Street Station, Lexington Avenue Subway,
New York, New York
Photos by M. Kamber

Val Carroll (p. 100)

Serendipidus I–IV
Photo by Raphael Salazar

Ann Gardner (p. 135)

Danza del Cerchio, Port of Seattle, Washington
Photo by Russell Johnson

Edith Kramer (p. 136)

Union Square,
14th Street Subway, New York, New York
Photo by Douglas Buebe

Jane Muir (p. 112)

Fruiting, detail
Photo by D. Mocatta

Shel Neymark (p. 138)

Rosalie Doolittle Fountain,
Rio Grande Botanic Garden,
Albuquerque, New Mexico
Photo by Herb Lotz

**Lilli Ann Killen Rosenberg
and Marvin Rosenberg (p. 116)**

Children's Center Mural, Four Seasons,
Philadelphia, Pennsylvania;
Celebration of the Underground,
MBTA Park Street Station,
Boston, Massachusetts;
Rainbow
Photos by Ken Wittenberg

April Sheldon (p. 139)

Patio and outside fireplace, Carmel, California
Photo by John Casado

Gary Stephens (p. 54)

Song of Summer (Self-Portrait II)
Photo by Jay Daniel

Bobbing for Apples;
Frog Fountain with Halo of Bugs;
Song of Summer (Self-Portrait I);
Watermelon Merman
Photos by Charles Kennard

Robert Stout and Stephanie Jurs (p. 60)

The Pathway I
Albuquerque Museum, New Mexico
Photos by Alan Labb

Curved Surface, mosaic entryway;
Donnelly Library, Highlands University,
Las Vegas, New Mexico;
The Pathway II
Albuquerque Museum, New Mexico
Photos by Norman Johnson

Zoe and Steve Terlizzese (p. 141)

Home Sweet Home and Clock of Ages
Photos by Richard Graulich

Isaiah Zagar (p. 126)

Kater Street Studio (South Street side);
Pemberton Street Wall;
Mildred Street Wall;
Photos by Barry Halkin

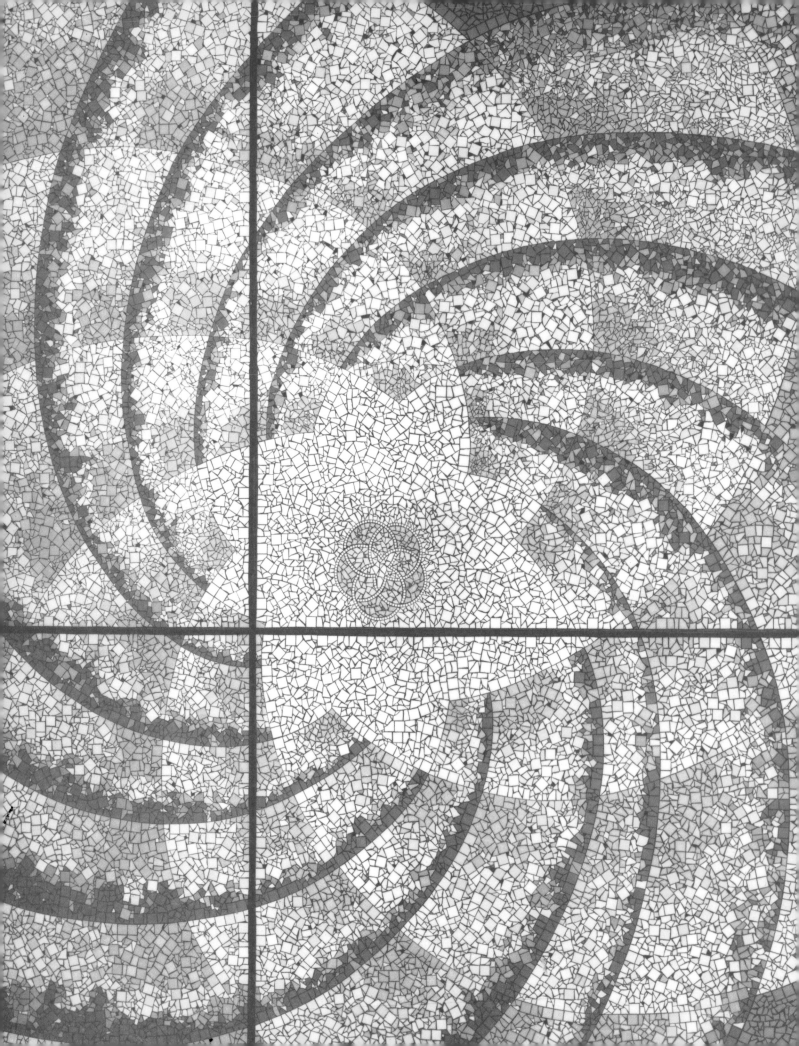